ACKNOWLEDGEMENTS

The translator wishes to express his thanks to Dr Christine R. Barker and Dr Alan D. Best for checking the typescript and reading the proofs. Any errors that remain are my own.

NOTE

Numbers in brackets in the text and notes refer to the four volumes of Hochhuth's work listed in the bibliography at the end of this book.

MODERN GERMAN AUTHORS
New Series

EDITED BY R. W. LAST

VOLUME FIVE

ROLF HOCHHUTH

by

RAINER TAËNI

Translated from the German
by
R. W. Last

OSWALD WOLFF
London

MODERN GERMAN AUTHORS—NEW SERIES
ed. R. W. Last

ISBN Cloth   0 85496 057 0
Paper   0 85496 058 9

© 1977 Oswald Wolff (Publishers) Limited
London W1M 6DR

MADE AND PRINTED IN GREAT BRITAIN BY
THE GARDEN CITY PRESS LIMITED
LETCHWORTH, HERTFORDSHIRE
SG6 1JS

CONTENTS

PART ONE

INTRODUCTION

I

THE LINKS BETWEEN LIFE AND WORKS

With his very first drama, Hochhuth created an international sensation, and the plays that followed equally
inspired heated controversy and even enmity in some
quarters. None the less, these works were not written
with the intention of sparking off the sensations they
invariably caused. There is no reason to disbelieve
Hochhuth when he states that, when he was working on
the material for *The Representative* (*Der Stellvertreter*)
and making up his mind on the most effective form for
the work, it never once occurred to him that it would
have the kind of impact it did. When he showed extracts
of the manuscript to friends, he adds, he was astounded
at the cautionary note they struck.

This unassuming modesty bordering on the naïve is
a key quality of Hochhuth the man. When he sets to
work on a subject which he considers important, it is
with a serious-mindedness directed at the subject-matter
alone. Even when still at school, he was clear in his own
mind that he was going to become a writer. His fascina-
tion with creative writing far outweighed any interest in
what school had to offer—which would hardly surprise
any German who can cast his mind back to the teaching
methods and curricula of the war years. His love of
writing was matched only by his voracious appetite for
reading. According to Dieter Vollprecht, the son of
his very first employer, he was seldom to be seen in
those days without a book in his hand.[1] His narrow

circle of friends consisted of a handful of like-minded boys.

At the tender age of fourteen, he fell under the spell of Thomas Mann; the speech through which Hochhuth first came to know this hitherto banned writer made an abiding impact upon him, as the novels and short stories were later to do:

> The sense of shame which this man inspired in a barely fourteen-year-old member of the Hitler youth when he spoke on the one hand of the solemn condolences expressed by the Japanese government at the decease of their arch-enemy Roosevelt, and in contrast to this of the Führer's broadcast on the death of 'the greatest war criminal of all time', has stayed with me throughout the past thirty years. When I heard those words spoken, it was a burning hot April afternoon, but I found myself shivering.[2]

On his own admission, two experiences in particular were dominant among the early impressions of the young Hochhuth. The first was the countryside around the town of Eschwege, where he was born in 1931. There is scarcely a trace of this influence in his dramas and essays, but that can hardly be said of the second experience, namely, his encounter with the political and historical developments which in those days it would be hard for anyone to ignore.

The Hochhuth family with their middle-class background—his father had been a shoe manufacturer, and was subsequently a seed merchant and food wholesaler —escaped the direct impact of the horrors of Nazi rule and the war. Within the home, the family was anti-Nazi, and his parents' opposition to the régime helped to fashion Hochhuth's critical awareness of what was going on all around him in Germany. He served his time in the Nazi youth movement with little enthusiasm and without attracting the approval of his superiors. The entry of American troops into Eschwege on 3 April 1945 he regarded as an historical turning-point of the greatest possible import. From then on, he has never been able to understand why literature fails to give contemporary history the attention it deserves, since the great upheavals taking place in those days left a permanent mark upon him.

The young Hochhuth was impatient for his schooldays to come to an end; only German and history were able to capture his attention. After passing his lower leaving certificate, he became apprenticed to a bookseller at the age of seventeen, which naturally gave him plenty of opportunity for reading. He was particularly attracted to the writers and historians of the nineteenth and twentieth centuries: the brothers Thomas and Heinrich Mann, Robert Musil, Otto Flake, and the historians Burckhardt, Spengler and Treitschke. He also did a lot of writing on his own account: some poems, a story entitled 'The Housing Commission' ('Die Wohnungs-komission'), another story, 'Inventory' ('Inventur'), supposedly autobiographical but becoming increasingly less so as he grew increasingly dissatisfied with the form and kept changing it, and a novel, also autobiographical, in the form of letters penned by six people during the days of the American occupation: it took as its title *4 Victoria St. (Victoriastr. 4)*, the address of his parental home. The novel was never completed; the choice of an epistolary form points to the fact that he had found his natural mode of expression in dialogue, that is to say, the drama.

While he was working in a variety of university book-shops, Hochhuth was able to attend regular lectures on history, philosophy and literature as an occasional student. But he had neither the inclination nor the necessary qualifications to enter into academic life, and most of his real knowledge was acquired from intensive reading. He concluded his apprenticeship with the publishing house of Bertelsmann, where he had gained a position as publisher's reader. He soon realised that he needed to devote his mornings to writing, and the firm generously allowed him to work on a half-time basis.

It was while reading an historical account of Gerstein's forcible entry into the Berlin nunciate that he chanced across the subject for his first drama, and he began collecting material. As a reward for the great success of his edition of Wilhelm Busch, which very quickly sold a million copies (as was the practice, the editor did not receive a penny in royalties), Mohn, the director of the firm, financed a stay in Rome for Hochhuth and his wife. There he was able to examine a great deal of important material. Looking back, Hochhuth now finds it ironic that he actually wrote large sections of *The Representative* in the Vatican itself, in the German library, where he was left to his own devices.

Karl Ludwig Leonhard, who used to be in charge of production for Bertelsmann, had moved across to Rütten & Loening to run the business there, and he it was who printed a paperback version of *The Representative*. Although the book was never actually put on the market because the subject was regarded as too controversial, a proof copy was sent to Ledig-Rowohlt, and that is how the text came into the hands of the producer Erwin Piscator. Hochhuth is quite convinced that if Piscator had not been prepared to stage the play at the Freie Volksbühne in Berlin, he would never have had any of his works performed in the German theatre.

It is typical of Hochhuth the man that even today he is immensely grateful towards anyone who takes up the cudgels on his behalf or assists him in any way. This attitude of his is clearly reflected in what he has written about other people. It shines through every line of what he wrote on the occasion of Piscator's death, as well as in the obituary of his friend the sociologist LL Matthias, where he states explicitly: 'The last word I have to say before the great silence falls is: Thanks.' (III,41) This penchant for gratitude also emerges from what little this modest man of letters reveals of himself in his works. 'L'Impromptu de Madame Tussaud' (1968), supposedly a short story but really nothing of the kind, contains the strongest autobiographical references of anything he has so far published. It concerns a kind of encounter in a dream with Churchill, with whom he had been greatly preoccupied during the previous three years of work on *Soldiers* (*Soldaten*). Also present is Hochhuth's publisher, Ledig-Rowohlt, whom he regards as 'potentially a double' of Churchill because of certain unmistakable similarities between the two men. Time and again in the course of the narrative the images of these two figures blur into one another, as a result of which the reader, like the figure present called 'myself', is frequently unclear about which of them is being referred to. The bulk of the text is taken up with an encounter between Churchill, Ledig-Rowohlt and 'myself' in Madame Tussaud's waxworks in London.

At one juncture the first person declares to the wax effigy of the former Prime Minister that he did not venture to write a play about de Gaulle, because the latter had intervened personally to prevent the Cardinal of Paris from seeking to get the police to ban performances of *The Representative* in the French capital:

Churchill: So you are open to bribery?
Myself: Yes—on grounds of gratitude. And since,

sir, we have you to thank for the fact that our
theatres are no longer under the yoke of Nazi censorship, I wrote a play about you : I hope it hasn't completely destroyed my respect for you.
He laughs : All I'd say is that you've dragged it out
a bit ! (III,75)

Churchill's reference in the last line to the great length
of Hochhuth's plays is a typical piece of self-irony. At
another point he ironises the reserve he experiences in the
presence of respected and egocentric personalities when
the first person is constrained at one point to remind the
great man 'hesitantly, that in the first place I am still
alive and secondly I'm not a wax figure.' (III,72).

Hochhuth's unobtrusiveness as an individual, which
has always caused him to remain in the background, is as
attractive as it is unexpected in a writer of such international fame, and one moreover who has been the cause
of more than one huge sensation. Hochhuth's attitude
to his own fame has been quoted by Vollprecht in these
terms :

All the ballyhoo surrounding what people call the
celebrity ... has turned out in reality to be what I'd
always expected it was—a mishmash of prostitution
and perspiration.[3]

IIe does not go out in search of fame, rejects sensationalism of any kind, and hates to act out the part of
the famous man.

His gratitude towards others, which is one of the
cornerstones of his personality, goes hand in hand with
his strong sense of justice, which has always driven him
to take the part of the disadvantaged whenever the
opportunity presents itself. This sense of justice is one of
the motive forces in his dramas, but it is also to be found

time and again in his essays, speeches and letters to people in authority. One illustration of this is to be found in his obituary of the writer Otto Flake, whose cause he also took up personally in his capacity as a publisher's reader. We owe it to Hochhuth's editorial efforts that this long-forgotten writer of fiction appeared in 1958 in a new edition and led to a belated success for Flake just before his death. Another side to this feature of Hochhuth's personality is the generosity he shows towards all his friends and colleagues. More than a few actors and people backstage have been on the receiving end of his munificence.

These efforts on behalf of others underline his passionate nature, his ability to identify personally with the sufferings of others. Philipp Wolff-Windegg has drawn attention to this fact in relation to the première of Hochhuth's first play :

> A drama like *The Representative* can only be written by someone utterly obsessed with a passion for the truth, and also one who is capable of reliving himself the conflicts and sufferings of his protagonists . . . and clothing them in dramatic form. . . . If there is a play of our time which was conceived neither in intellectual calculation nor artistic intent, but in the compelling impulses of a deeply wounded, suffering, and—in the last analysis—perplexed spirit, then this is the work.[4]

It is not known whether Hochhuth himself has suffered in his personal life or experienced deprivation, except for the fact that he has a form of facial paralysis which has been troubling him since he was twenty and which cannot be concealed. But he would rather not talk about it; he is more concerned—and not infrequently embittered—by the lot of others who are truly incapable of helping themselves.

As his works demonstrate, Hochhuth always becomes very sharp and disconcertingly concrete wherever he sees injustice done and wrongs to be righted. But despite this, there is nothing of the moraliser or fanatic about Hochhuth, despite the claims of many of his critics. He is an avid raconteur—and also a good listener, always eager to hear anything new. His passionate nature makes him open to all the pleasures of the senses, and the last thing one could accuse him of is censoriousness or puritanical petty-mindedness, although there have been occasions when people have tried to do just that. Hochhuth's love poems bear eloquent testimony to the fact that he is also fully cognisant of the banality, the synthetic sensuality in what goes by the name of 'love'; one of his most successful poems 'Call it Love' ('Nenn's Liebe'), which concerns a relationship between two young people, touches on this very theme.[5]

Hochhuth himself is happiest when in the company of women, and least content when attending any kind of official cultural junketings. In seeking to arrive at a balanced view of Hochhuth, it is perhaps not inappropriate to take some account of personal knowledge of Hochhuth the man, not least because people are often irritated by the uncompromising fashion in which he puts across his views in his own works, especially in those areas where he finds himself in opposition to generally accepted ideas and conventional modes of thought. Small wonder, then, that Hochhuth has so many enemies among those who have only a nodding acquaintance with his works and no knowledge of the man at all. Many such people feel that they are the objects of a personal assault which they find all the more difficult to counter since Hochhuth has right on his side most of the time. It is all too easy for anyone who knows Hochhuth only from his works to pass a distorted and one-sided judgement on him. And this is exacerbated by what Vollprecht has called his proclivity towards 'sharp-tongued overkill'. But this too forms part and parcel of his uncompromising nature—Hochhuth is not slow to come to conclusions, which he does without fear or favour. This does not mean that he is unwilling to discuss his views; on the contrary, he is quite prepared to leave himself open to persuasion and revise his opinions accordingly. Most of his works have been years in the making, and as a direct result of this the views they express have all been carefully weighed in the balance.

Since the end of 1963, that is, since the première of his first play in Basle, Rolf Hochhuth has lived there with his family. In his first year in that city, there were angry demonstrations—a torchlight protest march against *The Representative*, which it was only possible to stage under police protection, with the house lights up. That did not prevent seventeen performances from being given before sold-out houses. Despite this unfortunate beginning, he has stayed loyal to Basle. None the less, the doubt remains as to whether he ever will make a duly subservient Swiss citizen. And that is certainly no bad thing, least of all for the German-speaking theatre.

II

HOCHHUTH'S BREAKTHROUGH INTO THE POST-WAR GERMAN THEATRE

The unexpected success which attended Hochhuth's first play, *The Representative*, which turned him overnight into an international celebrity in 1963, cannot be explained simply in terms of its sensational subject-matter. One factor which certainly contributed to the play's impact was the fact that it filled two gaps in the theatre.

In the first place, as far as the 'message' is concerned, it touched for the very first time on an extremely sensitive taboo area. The very assertion in public that the blame for the terrible injustices meted out against the Jews under Hitler was not entirely to be laid at the door of the Germans was quite enough to create an uproar. The universally accepted view at the time was that Hitler and the Nazis, and the Germans at large, were solely responsible for everything that was done to the Jews in those days. But here was a dramatist, and a German one at that, stating quite unequivocally that even the Pope, the highest spiritual authority in the western world, bore some measure of responsibility for those atrocities.

In the second place, there was a real dearth of new German political dramas on the German stage in the early 1960's. It is true that between 1960 and 1963 the theatres had been opened up to new German writers, probably for this very reason. At that time it was possible for totally unknown writers to have their works staged by West German or Berlin workshop theatres; and for a brief while it really did seem to be the case that, alongside the producers, actors and set designers, the dramatists themselves were on the point of making a real contribution to the German theatre. But even in a climate so pre-eminently favourable to the dramatist, it was almost impossible for plays as explicitly political as Hochhuth's first work to find a theatre or a publisher. And it really is doubtful whether *The Representative* would ever have seen the light of day if it had not come into the hands of such a famous producer as Erwin Piscator.

The vacuum in the German theatre of that time was

an indirect consequence of the Nazi period, when the theatre was gagged and excluded from all outside influences. When the war came to an end, it is not surprising that, in West Germany at least, the theatre more or less rested content with filling in the gaps, so to speak, by establishing contact with the developments that had been taking place elsewhere in the theatrical world. The favourite writers of the 'fifties were Anouilh, Sartre, Giraudoux, T S Eliot, Christopher Fry, Hochwälder and Brecht, and later Frisch, Dürrenmatt, Beckett and Ionesco.

By about 1960, however, the theatre really seemed to have caught up; and then there began an intensive search for works by up-and-coming native talents. At the opening of the 1962–1963 season, the critic Günther Rühle was able to write that 'the dramatists have now been given the initiative'.[6]

The German dramatists of that period were men like Leopold Ahlsen, Herbert Asmodi, Tankred Dorst, Richard Hey, Peter Hirche, Claus Hubalek, Heinar Kipphardt, Siegfried Lenz, Hans Günter Michelsen, Hermann Moers, Erwin Sylvanus, Dieter Waldmann, Martin Walser and Konrad Wünsche. Many, if not most of them, had first made a name for themselves as poets, prose writers or radio dramatists. And in fact their works for the live theatre were in the main lyrical and symbolical, and if they made reference to the social and political realities of the day, it was only in an oblique and disguised form. Heinar Kipphardt's broadly realistic war play, *The General's Dog* (*Der Hund des Generals*), constituted a solitary exception to this general rule.

Only two other plays made a more or less explicit attempt to deal with the Nazi régime, and they were by men who had previously had some success as writers of narrative prose: *The Age of the Innocents* (*Zeit der*

Schuldlosen; 1960) by Siegfried Lenz, and *Oak and Angora* (*Eiche und Angora*; 1962) by Martin Walser. But, in the last analysis, both plays fall short by transposing historical fact on to a generalised symbolical plane. And this is the case even for the more realistic passages in the Walser play. The sharp edge of the Nazi horror is blunted either by symbolism or comic devices. Even the most important German-language drama at that time, the parable *Andorra* by the well-established Swiss author Max Frisch, suffered from the fatal flaw of failing to be specific in relation either to the time or place of the action.

Hochhuth's *The Representative*, then, was an innovatory piece of dramatic writing, both in its directness and specific political references. At first, this must have had a disconcerting effect on a theatre utterly unaccustomed to such fare. In any event, when Piscator demonstrated beyond doubt the significance of the work by giving it its première in Berlin, Hochhuth was at once established as a dramatist. There was no shadow of doubt that his subsequent plays would also be performed, however they turned out. For all that, *The Representative* was only produced on a handful of occasions in West Germany itself.

Nonetheless, Hochhuth's first drama had succeeded in making a breakthrough in the direction of political engagement in contemporary drama. The vogue for lyricism and a shroud of symbolism soon yielded place to a greater willingness to accept the representation on stage of more concrete subject-matter, even material that was politically highly charged. Plays like Martin Walser's *The Black Swan* (*Der schwarze Schwan*; 1964) and Hans Günter Michelsen's *Helmet* (*Helm*; 1965) were already showing indications of a more positive move towards concreteness of presentation than had the previous works of these two dramatists. It would, of course, be wrong to attribute this to the direct influence of *The Representative*; but there is no mistaking the influence of Hochhuth's first drama on the 'documentary theatre', both in relation to the employment of material drawn from the recent past and also the concern with topical issues. Among the important documentary dramas of the years that followed were *In the Matter of J Robert Oppenheimer* (*In der Sache J Robert Oppenheimer*; 1964), *Joel Brand* (1965), and Peter Weiss's play about the Auschwitz trial, *The Inquiry* (*Die Ermittlung*; 1964).

But it is as well to treat convenient labels like 'documentary theatre' with a fair measure of caution. The term hardly applies to Hochhuth's dramas, a fact which he himself stresses : he regards himself as a writer who accords 'the imagination its rights', even in the historical drama, and this means admitting 'things which the "pure" documentary play would exclude, namely, the invention of characters, transposing historical events from one place to another', and the like.[7] In Hochhuth's estimation, the judicious selective invention of individual characters does not do violence to historical truth. In this context he follows the precedent of Schiller's *Wallenstein* and Thomas Mann's maxim : 'One should not seek to make something out of thin air, but make something out of things'.[8] So he regards himself as a writer of historical rather than documentary dramas; but that has not prevented his works from exercising an influence on the documentary drama proper.

Similar difficulties and contradictions come to light if one tries to consider Hochhuth's work in the context of Brechtian theatre. There is no disputing the fact that there were very few dramas in the years 1960–1963 which seem more closely linked with the intentions of Brecht than *The Representative*. Just before his de in 1955, Brecht emphatically insisted that the world could only be shown to contemporary man in terms of 'a world that can be changed'. This *potential* for change is adapted by Hochhuth just as forcibly into a *necessity* for change. Yet he himself once stated that he deliberately set out to avoid falling under the influence of Brecht. He gave two reasons for this: first, Brecht the dramatist represented such a high-point in the theatre that to be exposed to his influence would be to be smothered by it;[9] and, secondly, Brecht's theatre was not concrete enough for him. In this context, Piscator personally warned Hochhuth insistently against Brecht:

> In the first conversation he had with me, Piscator . . . said he had previously come into conflict with Brecht and had told him: 'You write fairy-tale pieces; you ought to write about the political here and now instead of seeking refuge in Caucasia, Setzuan or in the past.'[10]

Hochhuth, of course, deliberately refrains from stylising the action by transposing it to other countries or historical periods. In both time and setting, his plays—in contrast to those of Brecht—are always close to the audience. In depicting historical events, he is simply and solely concerned with what he describes as the 'distillation' of reality, which involves the removal of all those things not directly pertinent to his theme.

But it is in the depiction of the protagonists that Hochhuth's dramas differ most sharply from Brechtian theatre. Their most distinctive quality, which sets them apart from all the prevailing styles and fashions of the time, is the fact that they are composed of two disparate elements: although they are 'epic' in the Brechtian sense, they display very basic 'un-epic' features which in the traditional sense of the term can be called 'dramatic'.

These will be explored in greater detail when the dramas
are considered individually. Their epic aspect derives
from the fact that they are unmistakably rooted in their
own time: they have a close and precise relationship
with historical events outside the context of the drama
which is unfolding on stage and entirely independent of
it.

Nothing would be more alien to Hochhuth than to
seek to heighten the dramatic impact of the events he
is depicting by resorting to the grotesque, let alone the
absurd, which he firmly rejects:

> I take ... the view that the so-called Theatre of the
> Absurd—I reject the term, and have dubbed it instead
> 'theatre of the abstract'—is the truly reactionary
> theatre of our time.[11]

This is not a blanket accusation—he excludes Beckett
from such charges—but he does direct it against Ionesco
and his imitators.

It is a generally accepted fact that, in the context
of contemporary works for the stage, the term 'drama'
has more or less lost its validity: it has been replaced
by the word 'theatre', whether epic, absurd, documentary, or whatever. What this implies is that, in contrast to the classical 'drama', the present-day stage
employs the whole gamut of 'theatrical' techniques—
including the grotesque, the absurd, Brechtian songs or
circus tricks—in performances whose alienated form
corresponds to the alienation of modern man. It is at
this particular point, setting aside the way in which a
play might be staged, that Hochhuth parts company
with these trends in the theatre; and this is where the
'un-epic' aspect of his work is to be found. So on the one
hand he holds himself aloof from Brechtian theatre, and

on the other from its opposite pole, the Theatre of the Absurd.

It is the picture of humanity presented by Hochhuth which gives his dramas their unique shape. In many respects, it is plain 'old-fashioned'. The critic Joachim Kaiser, writing a few years before *The Representative* was first performed, stated that 'the idea of man as a personally responsible individual is now a dream'.[12] In these words, Kaiser is seeking to express why it is impossible to reconcile Aristotelian drama with the depiction of contemporary events. Hochhuth utterly rejects any such assertion; in an answer to a questionnaire in 1963 from the journal *Theater heute* on the question 'Should the theatre depict the contemporary world?' he wrote : 'The fundamental objective of drama is to insist upon the fact that man is a responsible creature.' (III,3–9) So Hochhuth insists on restoring the 'dramatic hero' to the stage, however loudly the critics may proclaim from the rooftops that such a thing fails to do any justice to the realities of contemporary life. Hochhuth refutes this charge, on the grounds that he is concerned not with abstract symbolism, but rather with the concrete representation of historical reality.

Hochhuth's insistence on the responsibility of the individual helps to explain why it is that his basic line of approach to dramatic writing is so decisively un-Brechtian, and why it almost deserves to be called 'conservative'. His attitude owes little to current trends and fashions, to which he pays scant regard. This was a unique feature of *The Representative* in the early 'sixties, and has continued to be part and parcel of all his subsequent works to date. Not unnaturally, it has caused considerable offence; it has not only made it difficult for other dramatists to come to terms with Hochhuth, but it has also been instrumental in his blunt rejection by many critics and people in the theatre. Controversial themes, it appears, are less unpardonable than a supreme disregard for every rule and development in the theatre which the theoreticians have only just pronounced to be binding. And it must be a source of even greater annoyance among such folk that, despite all this, Hochhuth has been an unqualified success as far as the public is concerned. Nothwithstanding his position as an outsider, he has remained until the present day one of the few truly significant German dramatists of the post-war era.

PART TWO

THE WORK

I

INTRODUCTION : HOCHHUTH'S VIEW OF HISTORY AND POLITICS

Hochhuth's preference for the 'historical' as opposed to the purely 'documentary' theatre and his insistence upon the responsibility of the individual are intimately bound up with his conception of the function of the theatre and also with his outlook on life which underlies all his work.

The themes of his plays are based almost exclusively on a study of historical or contemporary material, including reports in the serious press, especially the news magazines. Such a study, if undertaken intensively, inevitably leads one to draw certain general conclusions about life which, in their turn, have an impact on the way in which the subject itself is treated. It has also left a decisive mark on Hochhuth's conception of the nature of the historical drama and of the function of the political theatre. Most important, his studies have led him to adopt an attitude of great humility towards their object, namely history itself. In this respect, he sees himself in a different light from other writers :

> Perhaps I am the first playwright who persists in the view that we are *not* entitled to handle history just as we please. Lessing wrote that the poet was the master of history—but I have always considered myself to be its servant.[13]

It goes without saying that this 'servant of history' feels

obliged to follow the teachings of history faithfully and, whenever necessary, to act as their advocate.

Almost everything Hochhuth has written reflects these preoccupations. His essays, political and non-political alike, reveal him not only as a writer who takes political engagement seriously but also as one who aspires to see the lessons of history gaining general acceptance. This is given equal prominence in the dramas themselves, and is to be seen especially in the extremely comprehensive stage directions and notes accompanying the text, which lend the plays something of the character of 'dramas for reading'.

For Hochhuth, the first lesson of history is that it is not possible to better human nature. Hochhuth utterly rejects the notion of humanity in some way evolving and striving towards the attainment of some ultimate objective. This places Hochhuth on the other side of the fence from the proponents of Christian salvation on the one hand as well as the supporters of a Marxist utopia on the other. Instead, he espouses the views of Oswald Spengler, the philosopher of history who regards the history of mankind in terms of a chain of recurring evolutionary patterns—as a continual sequence of cultures, each of which gradually moves towards a climactic point, only to go into decline and yield place to a new culture. Such are the sentiments behind the poem 'Study of circulation' ('Kreislaufstudie') in which Hochhuth envisages empires built upon sand :

> Denn nicht vorwärts, aufwärts nicht in Stufen
> Sondern in die Fläche wuchert weiter
> —und es wechselt wie die Kleider
> Nur die Rassen—, das Geschlecht des homo faber.
>
> (III,93)

(For not forwards, upwards, nor in stages / But on one

level grows rankly on / —and like changes of clothing/ only the races change—the tribe of homo faber.) Of the handful of poems which Hochhuth has published to date, those gathered together under the title *Leaves from an historical Atlas (Blätter aus einem Geschichts-atlas)* expand upon this conception of the nature of history. As a poet, Hochhuth is not outstanding, but the themes of transience and recurrence do lead him now and again to achieve unexpected and powerful formulations. These themes also run through the cycles *Privatissime* and *Travel Notes (Reisenotizen)*, where one of the poems ends with a reference to the vicious circle of human life ('Teufelskreis humanae vitae' : 'Lebenslauf'; III,429); another states that the poet too will be left without a trace ('Spurlos verläßt du auch mich' : 'Geh'; III,432); and another—from *Privatissime*—begins with these words on the cyclical nature of history :

> Städte der Griechen
> an den Ufern Siziliens
> aus euren Gezeiten
> aus euren Geschicken
> spricht unsre Zukunft.
> > 'Selinunt'; III,486)

(Greek towns / on the shores of Sicily / from your times past / from your fates / speaks our future.)

Significantly, Hochhuth's longest and certainly most important essay begins with a challenge to Herbert Marcuse and his assertion that a new and better society is possible in the future.[14] According to Marcuse, here quoted by Hochhuth,

> all that needs to be done is to develop the distorted instincts and drives of modern man in the direction of the needs of a society at peace. (III,354)

But this would require the 're-programming' of man, a fundamental change in human nature. Hochhuth regards this as an impossibility, because it stands in direct contrast to all the lessons of history :

> The idea that nature can be pacified has no basis in history, despite Marcuse's bold assertion, which he makes because he is no historian. (III,354)

So Hochhuth regards the notion of a pathway leading through an ever brighter future towards salvation as a pernicious illusion, an ideology which falsifies the nature of reality. This is why Hochhuth will have no truck with any views of this nature, whether they originate from Christians at one extreme or Marxists at the other. Like Dr Wiener, one of the characters in *Guerillas*, Hochhuth admits that he is 'scared rigid, first of all of history, and secondly of ideologies of any kind.' (III,355)

Nevertheless, Hochhuth—again like Dr Wiener—is 'naturally on the left, like any decent individual in a starving world', (III,355) but this does not necessarily involve commitment either to Marxism or Marcuse. Hochhuth does, however, share their view that the world needs to be changed—and that holds true just as much for socialist societies as for capitalist countries. And Hochhuth is equally insistent that the necessary changes cannot be wrought by piecemeal reforms, only by total revolution.

Does this mean that Hochhuth is a revolutionary? This is so in the sense that he does indeed believe in the necessity for revolutionary change, but Hochhuth does not believe that, given present circumstances, revolution can be carried through in practical terms. As he said in conversation :

> I am convinced that reform—or even revolutionary

change—can only be realised in a modern industrial society on the basis of infiltration.[15]

Hochhuth's play *Guerillas* seeks to put across this thesis in dramatic terms. And in his reply to a questionnaire on the issue 'Has revolution a chance in the Federal Republic?' he underlines his scepticism by stating that there is in West Germany a total lack of any kind of revolutionary spirit. There is, Hochhuth argues, no mass basis for revolutionary change; and on the other side of the coin, there are no intellectuals, no 'men of ideas, ready to risk their lives, let alone their jobs'. (III,351)

According to Hochhuth, the only opportunity for decisive change lies in a 'systematic infiltration' of the ruling oligarchy 'by men of decency'. (III,348) He stresses that the infiltrators would inevitably have to make the kind of compromises that great statesmen—like Churchill or Lenin, for example—would also have been courageous enough to make. The intellectuals would have to venture forth from their evangelical ivory towers and undertake the long uphill task of getting their hands on the reins of power, for example, by winning voters over to their side. Only then would they be in a position to bring about the necessary changes in society, such as are planned by the members of the conspiracy in *Guerillas*.

So this is not the scenario for a revolution in the classical sense of the term, but rather a revolutionary process initiated from above. Hochhuth's argument that there is no other possible approach has more than a ring of plausibility. The decisive factor is that the necessary action has to be undertaken by committed individuals dedicated to the common good. Hochhuth is well aware of the utopian streak in the line of his argument; he is fully cognisant of the fact that if in practice such individuals were ever to get to key positions of power they would inevitably fail for a variety of reasons—but he takes the view that it is essential for the venture to be undertaken, despite all the obstacles.

By and large, Hochhuth's theoretical writings mark him out as a somewhat unorthodox individual, in that he can be described as a pessimistic leftist with conservative tendencies. This might seem to be a contradiction in terms, but his position is in fact quite consistent.

His pessimism owes its origin to his unprejudiced and unblinkered view of history. Perhaps the most important lesson he draws from his historical researches is that, at the end of the day, all human endeavour comes to nothing :

> Jahre, 'Taten'—an den Wind verloren.
> In den Wind gearbeitet ! —klagt Salomo.
> Hekatomben hat Geschichte weggeschoren,
> wüstgelegt, genarrt, von nirgendwo
> und um nichts nach nirgends deportiert.
>
> (III,91)

(Years, 'deeds', —lost in the wind. / Written on the wind ! laments Solomon. / History has cut away catacombs, / laid them waste, duped them, from nowhere / and for nothing deported to nowhere.) But the pessimism which grows out of such an awareness does not cause him to give up the struggle and throw in the towel. Hochhuth turns for support to another pessimist, Ludwig Marcuse, with whom he feels a marked affinity, in contrast to his attitude to Ludwig's namesake Herbert. Hochhuth states that Ludwig Marcuse has demonstrated

> that it is the pessimists who have turned out to be the most politically active fighters and revolutionaries. They man the barricades for the very reason that they are aware of the wickedness of man and the evils of

power. They have less hope, but they fire more shots in anger than the others. (III,359)

Among such men, whom Ludwig Marcuse also cites, Hochhuth includes figures like Büchner and Byron.

In the light of this admission, it is clear that each and every revolutionary undertaking is a Sisyphean enterprise, an unending challenge, one that has to be started afresh over and over again. But, as Hochhuth points out, 'having to set Sisyphus' stone in motion . . . provides the inexhaustible fuel for the engine of the human comedy'. (III, 421) In other words, the action is meaningful in itself despite the fact that the ultimate outcome can never be positive.

The conservative element in Hochhuth's conception of the evolution of mankind is not so much to be found in his blank pessimism as in the conclusions to which that pessimism leads him : namely, that only the individual has any real possibility of undertaking constructive actions with the object of bringing about changes in society. Hochhuth regards it as self-evident that no such actions can have enduring results : 'No objective can extend beyond the life-span of a single generation, the impetus is not upwards, simply onwards'. (III,370) Such constructive actions, which seek not to establish enduring values valid for all time, but only to serve the interests of the present generation, are inevitably inspired by moral considerations. And this is something that can only be achieved by the individual, never by the mass.

At this juncture, it would of course be possible to put forward the Marxist objection that the history books constitute a crude falsification of reality, since they are essentially concerned only with describing the actions of individuals. Hochhuth, however, is well aware of the

objection, and is ready with a counter-question : What
does unfalsified reality actually look like? Hochhuth
shares the view of Karl Jaspers that man can never
aspire to attain a total and completely consistent view of
the world. Even an outline of the great historical movements to which the broad mass of humanity has been
exposed would not constitute a total picture of the world.
So Hochhuth adopts the approach of the historian
Burckhardt by taking the view that the sole tenable
standpoint for the observation of history is that of 'the
consistent individual'. (III,384)

In Hochhuth's estimation, revolutionary action must
also take due account of the individual if it is to remain
credible in human terms :

> Humanity only exists ... where man is regarded as an
> individual, not as a member of a group. The mass only
> exists insofar as it is the sum total of the individuals
> which constitute it. (I, 44)

Each of Hochhuth's dramas reflects this attitude, and in
this regard at least they appear to exemplify 'conservative' thinking, since it surely contradicts every 'modern'
and 'progressive' notion for someone to persist in stressing
the responsibility of the individual who has long since
been pronounced dead and buried by our technological
bureaucratised mass society.

The thesis underpinning Hochhuth's dramas, namely,
that even today the individual is still capable of initiating
decisive changes or even of making history, seems still
more anachronistic, as does his insistence on judging
such historical actions in moral terms, that is to say, in
relation to the characters of the individuals involved.

But it is more than a little unfair to write Hochhuth
off as a latter-day conservative. He describes himself in
these terms :

I too am an idealist—but a materialistic one, who ...
does not pour scorn on what is after all the most
important thing for mankind—the material world.
For do we not live but once and briefly at that?
(III,371)

Such an attitude is anything but conservative. In practice, this means on the one hand that Hochhuth, like
everyone on the left, regards the redistribution of wealth
as a necessity; but on the other hand, in contrast to most
politicians, he does not see the problem simply in
economic terms. On the contrary, he insists that it is 'a
moral issue'. (I,48) In essence, then, he is preoccupied
with a completely new vision of society, which in practice presupposes an entirely different political system, in
which politicians would have to be aware of the moral
dimension, although their options for practical action
still remained within the compass of economic restraints.

The essay which closes with the above sentiments bears
the title 'The Class Struggle is not over' ('Der Klassenkampf ist nicht zu Ende'). It was published in the weekly
Der Spiegel on 26 May 1965. Hochhuth's critical
attitude to the social policies of Erhard brought on his
head the violent wrath of all the conservatives and many
others in the establishment. It was this that caused
Erhard, the then Federal Chancellor, to coin the now
famous tag about 'the little terrier':

I have no inclination to trade words with Mr
Hochhuth on the subject of economic and social
policies. In my view, it is all foolish nonsense. They
are talking about things about which they don't have
the remotest idea ... That's beyond the scope of
the writer, that's where the tiny little terrier begins to
snap.[16]

To take just one more example of the opprobrium heaped on him by the establishment : Senator Helmut Schmidt, as Hochhuth states, sought to use the writer Siegfried Lenz to prevent 'my essay from being included in the Rowohlt paperback which brought together pro-SPD texts by twenty-five writers under the title "Plea for a new Government or no Alternative" '.[17]

Hochhuth's own account of the reaction to his article in *Der Spiegel* ('The Discussion of the Challenge to Class Struggle'; 1971) is notable not least because it demonstrates the impotence of the writer in the Federal Republic, and at the same time the hostility to which everyone in the country who ventures to express un-orthodox opinions in public is exposed. Four years after the controversial article in *Der Spiegel*, Hochhuth also drew upon himself the undying enmity of many people on the left, this time with the essay on Marcuse, to which reference has already been made. It was written for the journal *Konkret* on the occasion of the 1969 Federal elections, and in this case his reaction to the hostile response was to expand his theme and broaden the base of his arguments.[18] In both the article on the class struggle theme and in the enlarged Marcuse essay, Hochhuth expresses his view of the world, his concep-tion of politics and his understanding of the task of the writer. He regards the writer as an individual who should fearlessly espouse what he regards as vital issues.

Thus it is that the supposed contradictions in Hochhuth's view of the world, in which revolutionary leftist tendencies go hand in hand with pessimistic and conservative inclinations, are apparent rather than real. In fact, Hochhuth's approach is both logical and con-sistent. In essence, he starts out from a conception of history as an alternating sequence of cultural eras. This means both that history is cyclical and, also, that it is impossible for an observer of history to formulate a consistent world view. The result is inevitably pessimism : there is no possibility of any onward or upward progression in the direction of a paradisical state where we will all live happily ever after. The 'old Adam' in man is, as history demonstrates, ineradicable. But it is for this very reason that moral commitment is essential in order to challenge this state of affairs and to strive to bring about changes in real terms. On moral grounds, this can only be achieved by the individual himself undertaking practical action. And, according to Hochhuth, this he can only do on behalf of the present generation, for the here and now. The consequence of Hochhuth's approach is that revolution is inevitably a continual process : it has to be fought for and achieved anew by each succeeding generation.

Hochhuth himself also practises what he preaches, with his radical demands about the necessity for striving to attain concrete and limited objectives. This can be seen not only in the themes of his dramas, but also throughout his prose publications, which in the main are concerned with related topics : with the necessity for a law relating to aerial warfare, or of a coup d'état, with the current situation in the USA or the position of the older generation of writers in West Germany, a concern which also manifests itself in obituaries he has written, the funeral orations for deceased writers, to Pope John or Erwin Piscator.

Hochhuth deserves his self-assumed title of 'materialist idealist' on the grounds of his consistent and passionate commitment to concrete objectives. Although based on a detached study of history, the political action of his plays is always directed at the here and now, not in terms of Herbert Marcuse's projection of a utopian future, at and on behalf of the living individual, not towards the faceless mass.

This stance is not so far removed from that of Marxist ideologists, and Hochhuth would probably not deny this himself. He may be wrong to refuse to accept the notion of an ultimate utopian objective, since it does not necessarily follow that to cherish such an ultimate objective inevitably implies the rejection of concrete and specific action. It is not unlikely that Hochhuth tends to identify 'ideologists' all too exclusively with the bigoted dogmatists of Marxism who can hardly be said to be the most significant representatives of that movement. Of its very nature, Marxism insists on a continual dialectic, an on-going interchange between such apparent opposites as individual and mass or real and ideal—and that also means between a vision of the future and actions directed at the present moment. Hochhuth once branded all the 'religious', as he called them—by this he meant both Marxists and Christians—as 'those who find the world unendurable if they cannot paint a picture of a future which is better than the present'; (III,371) but in so doing he is surely being unjust to all those who employ a utopian vision of the future simply and solely as a model, a yardstick against which to measure present actions.

But there is a further facet to Hochhuth's thought, which might be termed 'revolutionary impatience'; it is this which has driven him to be less than fair to those on the left who adopt a different stance from his own and which has impelled him in the direction of concrete action. It is no coincidence that this selfsame streak of extreme impulsiveness is characteristic of so many of his central figures, from Riccardo and Gerstein to Nicolson and Lysistrata. We indeed live 'only once and briefly at that', and anyone who does not rest content with seeking consolation in a better life beyond the grave or a utopian goal, but is prepared to accept the slim chance that individual action might possibly lead to positive achievement, is inevitably driven in the direction of active involvement. Hochhuth's pessimism is 'anything but fatalistic', (III,415) it is indeed the exact opposite of resignation in its affirmation of immediate action.

Thus it also becomes clear why, in his early dramas, Hochhuth was still writing 'tragedies' at a time when the theatre was dominated by Brechtian epic drama on the one hand and the parables of the Theatre of the Absurd on the other. Hochhuth finds the absurd lacking in concreteness, and Brechtian theatre inappropriate to the depiction of positive action on the part of individuals impelled by a moral impulse. The result of that action is almost inevitably failure; but here too there is room for a certain measure of consolation. In his ultimate destruction, the tragic hero experiences confirmation of his moral stand and achieves a moral victory of a kind over the forces threatening man which he has been struggling to overthrow.

II

PROSE WORKS

In conversation, Hochhuth once stated that the dominant influence on his creative writing was not exercised in the first instance by other dramatists, but by his study of the great German historians of the nineteenth century like Mommsen or Jakob Burckhardt. And even when he was starting out as a dramatist, he deliberately avoided coming to grips with a writer of the

stature of Brecht. This he justifies by referring to his
early days as a creative artist :

> I began as a novelist, a prose writer, and even as a
> schoolboy was so much under the spell of Thomas
> Mann that when I more or less managed finally to
> extricate myself, I took good care not to expose my-
> self to the potentially oppressive influence of the best-
> known German dramatist of the 'fifties.[19]

Certainly it appears something of a strange admission
on the part of a writer who is known by and large only
as a dramatist that he was decisively influenced by
Thomas Mann, but the detailed descriptive material
and marginal notes in the plays, with their deliberate
stylishness and long, involved sentences, can only point
to an influence of that kind.

Surprisingly, though, the early stories reveal far fewer
of these features than might have been expected.
Resignation, or the Story of a Marriage (*Resignation
oder die Geschichte einer Ehe*; 1959) is Hochhuth's
earliest published work. A second, revised and extended
version appeared in 1974 under the title *Interlude in
Baden-Baden* (*Zwischenspiel in Baden-Baden*). All the
essential features of the narrative are, however, present
in the first version.

It is couched in the form of a diary. On a sudden
impulse, a thirty-four-year-old woman by the name of
Gertrud leaves her husband, taking with her her two
children, one eight, the other ten. She had discovered
that her husband was having an affair with his assistant,
an attractive young girl of nineteen. In her diary the
woman reveals her feelings, explores the situation she
finds herself in, and casts her mind back over the past.

Hochhuth admirably captures the language of a disappointed and aggrieved woman who believes she can-

not forgive her husband's 'little lapse'. Most significantly, her strong sense of order has been utterly shattered; and her desire for a divorce is probably motivated by an attempt to patch this sense of order together again. To this end, she eagerly accepts the offer of assistance made to her by a lawyer who chances to be staying in the same hotel in Baden-Baden.

But, since her hurried departure, one past experience has been constantly on her mind, the recollection of which she has evidently been suppressing for eighteen long years. During the war, when she was sixteen years old, she had had an affair with a Major billeted with her family. Both were naturally aware that it could never become a lasting relationship. Now she is tormented by the memory, and as she commits her thoughts to paper, it dawns upon her that her lover was himself deceiving his own wife with her, and that she had deprived his wife of a last chance for them to be together. And now she is haunted by yet another thought, namely, that in her infatuation for the Major she had been denying love to her own boyfriend, who was more or less her age. Soon after, he was to die on the battlefield 'without ever having slept with a woman'. (III,29) The Major himself only survived for a few days after his departure.

Gertrud's entries in her diary about what was clearly the most emotionally formative period of her life run parallel to her description of the gradually deepening relationship between herself and Dr Hilmes, the lawyer. She notes down how she is beginning to fall under the spell of this man who himself was divorced many years before. At first only someone she needed to talk to, he soon becomes much more important to her. She wishes to please him as a woman and to be accepted by him as such: 'Dancing and flirting—how good they can be when you're a stickler for order like me. How all irony

fails you as soon as you're lonely, in need of love.'
(III,36) On the very evening when she recognises that
she too is capable of being led astray, 'and therefore
how much she is dependent on forgiveness', (III,38) she
leaves the hotel. Now she is aware of the fact that the
break with her husband is not necessarily final, although
in the process she has lost more than a few illusions.

In this short story, which takes as its theme a passing
marital crisis, Hochhuth touches upon some of the
fundamental problems of marriage. The background is
filled in by means of conversations between Gertrud and
Hilmes on this subject, together with accounts of legal
proceedings on relationships in other marriages. The
focal point of the narrative, however, is the personality
of the diarist herself. On the one hand, Hochhuth persuades the reader to identify himself with her, but on
the other hand he allows the reader to see from the very
outset that she herself shares a measure of the responsibility for the failure of her marriage. She entered into
marriage with an impulsive and passionate man as a
means of compensating for a certain inflexibility in her
own nature. True, her sense of order was a support for
him when times were difficult, but the fact that she was
so pedantic also makes it understandable that a man
like her husband in this situation would easily fall prey
to the charms of a reckless young woman, even if it were
only a passing fancy.

In places, the letter she writes to her husband from
Baden-Baden is openly vindictive, but it is characteristic
of this woman, who is contemplating what she sees as
the inevitable break-up of her home and marriage, that
she adds this postscript : 'Don't forget we need heating
oil, do see to the roses and make sure the swimming
pool is covered.' (III,13)

In her thorough way, Gertrud is of course well aware

of her own weaknesses and tries to combat them. But it is all part and parcel of her character that it is only during the present crisis, after it had been forgotten for years, that perhaps the most serious mistake she has ever made gradually becomes evident to her; reading between the lines, it becomes clear that the episode with the Major was suppressed by her innate need for order. So that she could live on without internal conflict, it was evidently necessary for her to obliterate all memory of her youthful spontaneity, of the fact that she could be carried away by her emotions and was ready and willing to be swept off her feet. It was this passionate element in her character that had to be repressed.

As a result, her present situation as a disappointed and aggrieved woman is, indirectly at least, partly a result of her past inability to cope with her first and intense experience of love other than by a ruthless denial of her own nature. The broken marriage is revealed as a consequence of her own emotional inadequacies; and this is what makes it to some extent characteristic of every marriage that goes on the rocks.

In his portrayal of Gertrud's situation, the young Hochhuth was already demonstrating his gift for psychological insight and for the depiction of complex human experiences and relationships. And indeed, he regards most of his figures, including the tragic 'heroes' of the plays, in terms of such relationships, as much victims of social institutions—in the present case, that of marriage —as of their own individual drives. And, for their part, the social institutions are just as much eroded by the psychological inadequacies of the individual as they in turn contribute to his sufferings. Above all, they ensure that the individual is continually being exposed to new situations of stress and painful experiences. For this reason, as we have known since Freud, the individual finds himself under constant pressure to suppress and sublimate his emotions. This prevents him from being his true self, and frequently from acting in a 'human' fashion. As a consequence of such conflict situations which can neither be acted out nor controlled in a socially acceptable manner, the individual tends to be aggressive, obdurate and unfeeling. Hochhuth himself appears very much inclined to regard such phenomena as an unalterable part of human nature. Statements he makes in his theoretical writings tend to confirm this supposition; but his creative works, like this first short story, make it clear that such emotional rigidity or misdirected passion are, in the last analysis, no more than reactions to an inability to come to terms with certain fundamental aspects of the human condition, and the institutions of society only serve to make matters worse.

When, in her despair at the state of her own marriage, Gertrud casts her mind back, perhaps for the first time in years, to her welcoming attitude to love when she was a sixteen-year-old, she suddenly becomes aware of how love and guilt are inextricably bound up with one another in a loveless world. Since love is the only true reality within the grasp of the individual, especially in times of extreme pressure from outside, people will tend to rush into one another's arms without a second's thought. Where religious faith has also failed, love is overwhelmed

far more strongly than ever before by all manner of inhibitions ... if an individual, who could seek consolation in God when he still had his faith, now sees in love his only refuge from the meaningless and sorry tale of his life that is threatening to tear him apart. (III,32)

Even in this early story, we can see the awareness of

history so characteristic of Hochhuth. At the end of the day, our realisation of the limited historical span of human life lends a certain depth and significance to the most intense of human experiences, and especially love. The Major, who deceived his wife with a sixteen-year-old girl, was doomed to die. He knew it—they both knew it—and this knowledge gave their love its special significance.

The motif of love as the most precious and meaningful thing left to man in the face of the constant threat of dehumanisation or destruction recurs time and again in Hochhuth's work. It is to be seen in the Auschwitz monologue by the Jewish girl in Act Five of *The Representative*: 'And do not tarry with love! Lovers are pursued, / and always in peril. Do not let your day slip past.' (II,177) Or in a note to *Soldiers*: 'Love is the last remaining unproblematical force in a situation where it is not the psychiatrist who is waiting by the bedside, but death itself.' (II,420)

It is when Gertrud calls to mind this insight which she gained during her affair with the Major that she finds her way back to her true self. Aggrieved jealousy is not the appropriate response to her husband's conduct, which was after all only human:

If I think back to my last hours with Ernst, then it seems to me that anything in the world that is done in the name of love can be forgiven. (III,34)

And in relation to her husband, she writes: 'I have realised for a long time that Fred and R. are no more guilty than Ernst and I were.' (III,35)

In the last analysis, life emerges as a more powerful force than any code of morality or a calculating search for order. But Gertrud is still incapable of changing her character; at the same time, however, she recognises that

there is precious little room for manoeuvre in her out-
ward life. So she returns to the semblance of order in a
marriage which she now recognises as the illusion it had
been all along. Since her resignation is founded upon
profound self-insight, it is not a negative act. What
happens here bears the promise of positive changes :
Gertrud begins to assimilate the estrangement of her
marriage into the totality of her life as a human being
and her development and experiences.

It is this close interrelationship between present
anxieties and the experiences of extreme situations in a
wartime past which gives this story its attraction. The
narrative technique fits the story line like a glove : the
style of the diary entries is, by and large, that of a very
precise, respectable and incorruptibly honourable woman
going in search of self-awareness and drawing up some
kind of account of herself. So there are none of Thomas
Mann's convoluted sentences, nor the tedious pursuit of
excessive detail such as is to be encountered now and
again in the marginal comments to the dramas; instead,
we find terse, graphic descriptions of the present situation, of thoughts, conversations with Hilmes, and the
like. But when it comes to recording the memories of her
youthful love affair, the style changes : there are frequent
long sequences of fleeting impressions jostling one
another, reflecting the breathlessness, the confused
emotion and the overwhelming force of her situation at
that time :

> Oh, on and on, then came the fir trees, it was so
> simple to ride along the woodland paths, the horse
> was swift and docile, I bent over its neck, my face
> brushed its mane, I loved it, I loved everything, again
> I touched its hair with my face, it flooded through
> me so warmly . . . (III,31)

In these lines she is recalling how she was swept along by the elemental experiences of life, to which she is now reaching back, after having wasted so many years holding them in check and suppressing them. It is in passages like this that Hochhuth demonstrates his gift for psychological observation; but they also reveal his sense of the tragic nature of life, the inevitable fact of approaching old age, the increasing burden of guilt, and the finality of death.

This tragic awareness of human life comes across even more forcibly in his second published work, the story *The Berlin Antigone* (*Die Berliner Antigone*; 1961). The very title contains a reference to Greek tragedy; and, just as in Sophocles' *Antigone*, the central figure is a young woman who scorns the power of the state and its threat to her life by burying her executed brother. The plot is taken from something that actually happened during the war in 1943. The narrative focuses on the inner conflicts of an individual caught up in an extreme situation. In spite of what she does, Anne, the central figure, is not especially courageous by nature. She had not reckoned with the fact that removing the body of her brother from the Berlin Institute of Anatomy—to which the bodies of the executed were conveyed during the Nazi period—could bring the death sentence upon her. However, when she stands before the court as a condemned woman, she is presented with one more chance; although the judge disapproves of her engagement to his own son, he is naturally anxious to save her life. He gives her time to reconsider her actions; if she returns the body of her brother she will be 'let off' with a term of imprisonment.

It is this situation which constitutes the source of the real conflict in the narrative. In the words of the judge's ultimatum to her, she is now 'no longer free of the fear

of death', (III,43) since Anne's desire for life is now in
direct conflict with her will to stand by her act of giving
her brother a last resting place. After a hard inner
struggle, she chooses death, and writes in a letter to her
fiancé who is fighting at the front that she 'would not
find it meaningless to die for what she had done'. (III,45)

> And in the end she even found a measure of tran-
> quillity in the banal thought that so many people die,
> day after day, without even knowing why—but she
> at least would have had that consolation. (III,45)

But this is not the whole story, and it is at this point
that the element of tragedy comes to the surface : Anne
is inextricably caught up in the web of consequences
that flow from her decision. The reason is that, after
she has taken leave of a fellow prisoner who is being
led out to execution, she suddenly realises that she

> was being cut off at a single stroke from what she had
> done; she no longer understood the girl who buried
> her brother, no longer wanted to be that girl, wanted
> to take it all back. (III,46)

But now that it once more becomes important for her
to live, it is too late. She cannot escape from her earlier
decision; and, when her fiancé receives her letter, he
shoots himself in order to be with her, since he supposes
her to be already dead. So it is now impossible for her
to retract what she has done; and she is executed.

This situation of an un-heroic heroine and her fateful
implication in the consequences of her own actions anti-
cipates a key theme of Hochhuth's 'tragedies'. But here
too we see for the first time the 'little people', the normal
folk 'like you and me', who in those days collaborated
and took upon themselves a measure of guilt. This does
not mean that they were evil, there were simply no other

options open to them, because if they opposed the state it would be impossible for them to maintain the image of themselves which they had employed all their lives as a mask of their hidden fears.

Hochhuth has demonstrated this aspect of human nature time and again in his characters. Wherever people assume guilt as a result of cowardly or unfeeling conduct, it is most often not the result of any innate wickedness; they have been driven to act in this manner by their own psychological defence systems.

The judge, however unwillingly, seeks to prevent Anne's death, and in the last analysis loses his son because of the selfsame terror machine which he himself serves. But he is incapable of escaping from it—on the contrary, he has become 'through frequent tears more faithful' to the already lost Nazi cause. (III,47) And the wardress—'a widow with many children, who secretly often used to bring Anne an apple' (III,48)—deprives her prisoner of the last chance of putting an end to her own life. After a pane of glass in the cell window had been shattered in an air raid, the wardress searches her prisoner thoroughly and finds 'the sharp fragments of glass which Anne had concealed in her hair under her head-scarf as a final weapon against her ultimate degradation'. Hochhuth describes the reaction of the wardress, which is far from unkindly, in these terms :

> She laughed heartily, the German matron, because she had been more cunning than her prisoner, she laughed without viciousness—and was so overcome when she saw tears in Anne's eyes for the first time, and was so totally unprepared to ward off her whimpering, despairing, insane pleadings for the glass splinters that she made a hasty departure to fetch her an apple. (III,49)

Anyone who has found a career, a rôle, a mode of life which gives them a *raison d'être*—in this case, the rôle of the 'maternal wardress'—is at the mercy of an inner compulsion to play this rôle to the limit, a drive which cannot be broken even by compassion for one's fellow creatures. That is why the woman tries to console Anne with an apple, after she has deprived her of her last shred of real consolation, and in so doing confirms her image of herself as a maternal being which has always been a source of inner security for her, but which has caused her to forfeit all links with true humanity.

Hochhuth's awareness that people fall into guilt as a result of such inner drives and not because they are wicked by nature lends his characters their credibility. This also holds good for the secondary figures in his works; in this regard, they are just as much human beings as the protagonists, the 'heroes'. They too are at the mercy of similar compulsions which by and large are responsible for their ultimate fate. But the central figures stand out in that they struggle against such drives, even in themselves; they also set their own self-image and defence mechanisms at risk, and strive courageously to break through to the truth. What the Antigone of Berlin hints at in this respect is often to be developed in the dramas.

III

THE REPRESENTATIVE

Hochhuth's first play, *The Representative*, was written between 1959 and 1961. After its première in February 1963 in the Berlin Kurfürstendamm theatre under the direction of Erwin Piscator, it became a world-wide success. But when first written, no one was prepared to publish or produce it. True, it was given a secondary award which formed part of the Gerhart Hauptmann prize—but not the major prize itself; and this was symptomatic of the hesitancy of the powers that be in the theatre, who were afraid to come to close quarters with this 'hot potato'.[20] They presumably held back for the very reasons that induced Piscator—who thirty years previously had made his name as the champion of Brecht and his 'epic theatre'—immediately to enthuse for the play : namely, the fact that it takes as its subject an extremely sensitive political issue. And at the time, the historian Golo Mann wrote :

> Indeed, it is to be wondered at how this work could . . . have been created in the stale atmosphere of West Germany, where once again the routine of self-righteous officialdom is sitting firmly in the saddle, face to face with an equally self-righteous and largely unproductive radicalism.[21]

What makes *The Representative* so polemical and politically provocative is its claim that Pope Pious XII was guilty of moral turpitude during the Nazi war when he failed to make any serious attempt to prevent the abduction and annihilation of the Jews. This charge is put into words by the Jesuit priest Riccardo, who is determined to pursue it further. The first four acts concentrate on his vain efforts to persuade the Pope to protest against the persecution of the Jews. He finds an ally in Kurt Gerstein, an SS-Obersturmführer, who believes that, by pretending to go along with the Nazis, he is best able to fight the régime and offer assistance to those who fall foul of it.

The very first scene places the entire issue squarely

before the eyes of the audience. First we see Riccardo,
who has just been transferred to Berlin, in conversation
with the papal nuncio. A discussion takes place on the
extremely difficult position of the Church in the capital
of the Reich in the year 1942 and its ambivalent attitude
towards Hitler. Then Gerstein bursts in unannounced,
to inform the nuncio of the gassing of Jews in Polish
concentration camps. The figure of Gerstein is true to
historical fact, as is his uninvited visit to the nuncio,
whilst Riccardo is a composite based on two historical
figures, Father Maximilian Kolbe and Lichtenberg, the
Berlin cathedral provost. The action takes an important
step forward when Riccardo recognises that Gerstein's
efforts are fruitless, and resolves to exert his own influence
in the matter. His father, Count Fortuna, who lives in
Rome, is a close confidant of the Pope, and this fact
gives Riccardo confidence in the outcome.

The second scene of the first act completes the exposition : here we meet some of the leading Nazis, among
them Eichmann, in the relaxed atmosphere of the
Jägerkeller hotel in Falkensee outside Berlin, where they
are drinking, playing skittles and also engaging in
jocular exchanges about Auschwitz and the Jews; and,
in the third scene, we witness Riccardo's visit to Gerstein,
who is anxious to support the priest in his endeavours.
Riccardo is still very confident of success : 'I can guaran-
tee you, Gerstein, that his Holiness will make a protest.'
(II,58)

But when Riccardo speaks with his father in Act Two,
the first doubts arise as to the eventual outcome of his
enterprise. The count explains that, for reasons of state,
the Pope is not a free agent, though naturally, using the
same form of words as the nuncio had previously
employed, his heart goes out to the victims. A cardinal
calls upon them, and Riccardo repeats his demands to

him. He even has a very precise notion of the form that the Pope's protest should take:

> Please don't try anything
> via Weizsäcker, nor via the nuncio,
> the Pope must go directly to Hitler! (II,95)

After an initial outburst of anger at such an unseemly proposition, Fontana and the cardinal shake their heads sadly over the gravity of this 'insoluble problem'. Although the cardinal had been summoned to the Pope to discuss a political issue, namely Stalingrad, it is quite clear that he has no intention of raising the Jewish question with him.

In the third act, Riccardo, this time with the support of Gerstein, makes a second initiative. This time he speaks to an abbot, who is known to be concealing refugees from the Nazis in his monastery. He expresses the resolve to go to Auschwitz himself to serve as the Pope's representative among the prisoners if his Holiness refuses to break his silence. And Gerstein even proposes that the abbot should step in in place of the Pope, and go on Vatican radio to call upon every priest in Europe to assist the Jews in their plight. In the end, Riccardo goes much further—he even entertains the notion that perhaps the Pope might be assassinated, and the SS blamed for the murder:

> No one, no Goebbels and no cardinal,
> could credibly deny it,
> before the crematoria of Auschwitz
> are extinguished. (II,127)

This idea the abbot naturally rejects out of hand.

In the fourth act, Riccardo finally succeeds in gaining a personal audience with the Pope. In the presence of his father, the cardinal and the abbot, he is once more apprised of the fact that, for reasons of state, it is not possible for any protest to be made. For all his short-comings, it is argued, Hitler represents a bulwark against Bolshevism, to which the Catholics of central Europe must never be delivered. And, when Fontana, albeit half-heartedly, defends his son, the Pope does go so far as to dictate a decree in which he testifies to his sympathy for all those who have fallen victim to the Nazi terror. But in doing this, he is so anxious to preserve his neutrality that he avoids any direct reference to the persecution of the Jews, even in Rome itself. Riccardo accuses the Pope of giving Hitler

> carte blanche
> to treat the Jews
> just the same as ever. (II,169)

But the Pope is anxious to preserve his status as an 'honest broker', and is fearful of antagonising Hitler. To the Pope's horror, Riccardo fastens the Star of David on to his soutane and rushes out. His resolve to join the ranks of the persecuted in Auschwitz itself is now un-flinching : 'God shall not bring ruin to the Church / just because a Pope fails to measure up to his vocation.' (II,171)

In its depiction of these repeated confrontations from the first to fourth acts, *The Representative* can almost be termed a *Stationendrama*; that is, a play incorporat-ing a series of scenes or 'stages' linked together by factors other than the development of a self-contained plot : for example, a particular character or theme. The scenes in which Riccardo advocates the cause of a papal protest increase in their dramatic intensity to a climactic point in the scene with the Pope himself. But this scene does not spell the end of the play itself. In the first place, there are between the main *Stationen* or 'stages' a number of other significant scenes which fill in the background to the main issue. Among these is the Jägerkeller scene in Act One, which not only shows the Nazis as 'human beings', in a relaxed, off-duty atmosphere, their plots and intrigues, and their psychological deformities, but also reveals the fact that they do take heed of the influence of the Catholic Church, of which they are even a little afraid. And it is in this scene too that the doctor is introduced, a figure who is to play a crucial rôle in the fifth act. He is the exception among this band of moral cowards and cringing lackeys; for he represents in a real sense the embodiment of evil itself, which makes him the true adversary of Riccardo and Gerstein. In other scenes, we see those persecuted by Hitler : the arrest of Jews in Rome; (Act 3, Scene 1) their interrogation by the Gestapo; (Act 3, Scene 3) and also a Jew whom Gerstein has been keeping in hiding, Jacobson by name, whom Riccardo tries to help by placing his soutane and passport at the man's disposal in order to assist his flight. (Act 1, Scene 3) In this scene, another link is forged with the fifth act : Riccardo's generous gesture turns out to be fateful for Jacobson, for when Gerstein attempts to bring Riccardo out of Auschwitz, where he had gone of his own free will, it is Jacobson who is brought before him instead. He had been arrested with Riccardo's passport on his person; and the final outcome of this involved situation is that Riccardo himself is shot by a guard.

The fifth act itself opens with a scene consisting of a number of monologues in which abducted Jews give voice to their feelings. Here, in stylised poetic language, the horrors of Auschwitz are emphatically brought home to the audience in terms of the human suffering it engenders. After the monologues, the audience is presented with a chillingly realistic sound-picture of these horrors : the opening of railway wagon doors, shouts of command,

screams and cries, the barking of dogs, all of which
convey an atmosphere of the terrifying confusion attending the arrival of a new batch of prisoners in the concentration camp. This scene more than refutes the frequent
assertions on the part of critics and theoreticians of the
theatre that it is not possible to portray Auschwitz on the
stage.[22] The fifth act is seldom performed, even in a
shortened version, and Hochhuth himself advises producers to use the Basle acting version of 1963. (II,271ff)
In this alternative version, the last act is replaced by a
revised Act 3, Scene 3, in which Jews are being interro-
gated in the Gestapo cellar, where Riccardo himself is
now being held prisoner. The original fifth act is, however, dramatic in the extreme: after the monologues
scene, the two ensuing scenes concentrate on the conflict
between the doctor and Riccardo. The critic Walter
Muschg even goes so far as to assert that the play 'stands
or falls by its grandiose final act'.[23] The real problem that
this act poses relates in the main to the question of how
it can be reconciled with the events previously depicted
on the stage. In a real sense, it creates a division in the
structure of the work, causing it to fall between epic
theatre on the one hand and classical *drama* on the
other.

Although Hochhuth's concept of history does not
permit *The Representative* to be regarded simply in
terms of the documentary theatre, Piscator had good
grounds for describing the work in his preface as 'epic',
as a

> play for an epic, 'political' theatre for which I have
> been campaigning for more than thirty years: a 'total'
> play for a 'total' theatre. (II,9)

By way of explanation, it ought to be pointed out that
the concept of 'epic theatre' sprang to prominence not so

much on the basis of Piscator's own productions in the 'twenties, but more especially as a result of Brecht's plays and theoretical pronouncements. Brecht regards the term as the direct opposite of 'Aristotelian' or 'dramatic' theatre. Drama, as defined by Aristotle, has a closed form, that is, it is detached from its audience, complete in itself and acted out in a world governed by its own independent laws. The audience only participates in the action to the extent of identifying with it on an emotional level. In a tragedy, this means by and large identifying with the sufferings of the hero. In Brecht's words, the feelings of a spectator in this situation go something like this : 'Yes, I've felt the same myself. I'm like that. . . . The sufferings of that man or woman move me deeply because there is no way out of them.'[24]

By contrast, the 'epic theatre' with its open form expressly involves the historical background to the events acted out on stage and frequently also calls upon the direct participation of both author and spectator. What is depicted on stage, then, is not a self-contained world in itself, but one that can be recognised as a reflection of external reality. Peter Szondi stresses as one of the main principles of the epic as opposed to the traditional dramatic form this open-ended link with external factors with which the author is dealing, as well as the absence of any kind of 'dialectic between people'.[25] What he means by this is that the action does not unfold as a causally related sequence of events within the drama itself, but reveals the dramatist as coming to grips with situations outside the immediate context of the work itself. And it is for this reason that relationships between characters are of less significance than the stance adopted by the characters to these external factors, which may be social or political in nature. According to Brecht, the spectator would learn something about his own place in the world and the wickedness of humanity. For this reason, the spectator must hold himself at a critical distance from the protagonists of the play he is watching :

> The spectator in the epic theatre says : that never occurred to me. —That's not the way things should be done . . . a stop ought to be put to that. —The sufferings of this man or woman move me deeply, because there is a way out of them.[26]

Distancing the audience on the emotional plane is achieved by means of 'alienation'. By interrupting the dialogue with songs, by displaying scene titles commenting on the action, by authorial observations which are clearly recognisable as such, and by incorporating cine film, transparencies, or sound material in the production, the spectator's tendency towards uncritical emotional identification is blocked and a strong link forged between him and the social reality outside the theatre. As Piscator stresses, *The Representative* is

> a thoroughgoing epic drama in the first instance because of the literary mould in which it is cast. The stage directions, production notes and personal descriptions of the characters, which are crucial to the work, are blended in with the dialogue to form an inseparable part of the drama itself. (The same holds true for the documentary appendix.) The wealth of facts in the text is heightened by the verse form of the dialogue. (II,10)

And indeed it is Hochhuth's intention to forge a link with external reality. The spectator is to be apprised of events that took place during the war years, of the persecution of the Jews, and of the relationship between the Vatican and Hitler. The intention is that the spectator should be persuaded to accept Hochhuth's thesis that the Pope should have sought to make a protest. There is no doubting the fact that Hochhuth is straining every nerve to convince the spectator that he ought to take a positive stand in regard to this issue. He even goes so far as to indulge in explicit criticism of characters portrayed on stage, which he makes it clear are drawn from life. Of the nuncio, for example, he writes:

His sympathetic face . . . refuses to make any kind of answer to the question of how this man of the cloth, who lived in Berlin throughout the whole of the Nazi period . . . managed to reconcile his conscience to the preservation of the concordat . . . even at a time when Catholic Jews were being deported. (II,13)

Or, in another context, he criticises a minor figure:

The Sergeant is called Witzel and, in 1943, looked like the majority of his fellow countrymen who were thirty-five years of age, just as he looks like the majority of those of fifty now he is a chief inspector of the city administration in D. (II,103)

The individual scenes are set in their historical context by being precisely located in time and place; for example, 'On the following morning, Gerstein's flat, Berlin W35', 'Rome, 2 February 1943, Fontana's house on the Monte Gianicolo', and so forth. On the other hand, even when they have historical prototypes, the characters are explicitly regarded as more or less interchangeable. In the list of dramatis personæ, they are put together in groups of two to four, all the characters in any one group to be portrayed by the same actor, on the grounds that

in an age of general conscription it is not necessarily a question of merit or blame—or even a question of character—whether a man or woman . . . stands on the side of the executioner or of the victim. (II,12)

This grouping of the characters also makes it less difficult
for the spectator to judge them critically rather than
identify with them.[27]

The choice of a verse form, not a stylistic device
normally associated with the epic theatre—after all, most
classical dramas are in verse—also serves the purpose of
alienating the spectator in that it inhibits emotional involvement. As Piscator indicates in his preface, Hochhuth
was endeavouring to steer clear of a 'bland documentary
naturalism in the manner of the weekly review' (II,10)—
that is, to prevent the spectator from identifying himself
with characters or action because of the topicality of the
language. For the same reason, Hochhuth later turns
against the alienation device much favoured by Brecht,
namely, cine projection : 'It's a relief that with this set
it is technically impossible to project a film of Nazi
victims on to the cyclorama.' (II,166) In this respect
too the choice of form is designed to assist the spectator
in taking the message of the drama to heart.

For all that, however, *The Representative* is by no
means an out-and-out Brechtian piece. In general,
Hochhuth goes out of his way not to fall under the
influence of Brecht, but the main reason why this play
differs from the Brechtian pattern is to be found in
Hochhuth's concept of the nature of history. Being convinced of the principle of individual responsibility,
Hochhuth is also anxious to stress this fact when he is
informing the audience about historical events, because
he regards these events as falling within the ambit of
individual influence.

It is true that there is some common ground between
the two dramatists where links between action on the
stage and external factors are concerned; by contrast,
relations between characters emerge as relatively un-
important in Brecht. In *Mother Courage* (*Mutter*

Courage), the external factor is war as an institution, illustrated by the example of the Thirty Years' War; in *Galileo Galilei* it is the Church; and so on. Brecht's criticisms are levelled against the manner in which his characters conduct themselves in relation to these external factors.

In *The Representative*, a similar situation is to be seen in the context of the Hitler régime and its persecution of the Jews. Hochhuth here seeks to demonstrate the failure of Pope Pius XII in the face of these circumstances, and to educate his audience to recognise this. But, in contrast to Brechtian theatre, the character exposed to this extreme criticism is not the central figure. The Pope only appears in one scene in the entire play, albeit an important one. Even then, he is seen entirely as a representative of the Catholic Church as a powerful institution. Unlike Mother Courage, Galileo or others of Brecht's central figures, we never get to see him in a situation of personal conflict, that is, as a 'human being'.

This is not so as far as Riccardo or Gerstein are concerned. These two men are the real central figures of the play, and Hochhuth nowhere exposes them to criticism. They are the only characters depicted who are not alienated from the audience, and they are virtually the only characters excluded from the groupings of characters to be played by the same actor. They are positive and responsible 'heroes' in the classical, Aristotelian sense.

Since Riccardo assumes the rôle of the critic in *The Representative*, there is no necessity for the dramatist himself to intervene. What Hochhuth has to say on his own account, as it were, is clearly expressed in the play by Riccardo, not within the context of alienation in the form, say, of Brechtian song, but spontaneously and directly, within the framework of the development of the drama itself. So it is Riccardo who expresses these criticisms of the Vatican in the scene with the Pope, as he does at numerous other points in the action :

> . . . When finally
> will the Vatican act in such a way
> that we priests are allowed once more
> to admit without shame that we
> are servants of that Church which in charity
> sees its highest commandment. (II,170)

There is to be found in *The Representative* a further feature not generally held to be significant by the epic theatre; that is, relationships between characters. Where such relationships occur in Brecht, they are completely subordinated to the critical intentions of their author. Naturally, *The Representative* is also primarily concerned with the attitude of the characters to external pressures, but not exclusively so. In fact, the incident which gave Hochhuth the idea for the whole play— Gerstein forcing his way into the nunciate[28]—is a self-contained exposition in the classical sense; that is to say, a complex initial situation which is capable of being developed in purely dramatic terms without any necessity for the dramatist to make any additions on his own account. The initial situation works itself out in this way : it is the personal example of Gerstein, which Riccardo witnesses in the nunciate (Act 1, Scene 1) which encourages him to take action himself. For this reason he seeks out Gerstein in his flat, (Act 1, Scene 3) where he also meets the infiltrator Jacobson. From this point, a further important strand in the action develops, one which is based on relationships between characters : as a 'demonstration of your good faith', Gerstein requests Riccardo to place his pass and his priest's soutane at the disposal of Jacobson, who is seeking to flee. (II,67) And this action in turn leads in the fifth act to Jacobson's fateful involvement in Gerstein's plan to free Riccardo from Auschwitz.

It is in the fifth act that the dramatic elements of the action come to a head. In a purely epic drama this final act would have had as little dramatic function as the figure of the doctor, who makes another appearance at this juncture. But the doctor is very necessary for Hochhuth, who is seeking to demonstrate his thesis relating to the responsibility of the individual : the doctor serves the purpose of deepening Riccardo's religious conflict which is entirely 'dramatic' in that it remains completely within the context of the action itself, and which makes it appropriate to the 'tragic' hero.

It is at this point that it becomes most clearly evident that the drama is divided against itself, since Hochhuth does not rest content with criticising the Pope, but incorporates into his drama the thesis of the responsibility of the individual in order to underline his theme. As a result, 'tragic' elements have been transplanted into an 'epic' situation.

In the programme notes to the première, *The Representative* is described as a 'Christian tragedy', and this description also heads the 1967 edition. And, indeed, Brecht's account of the emotional involvement of the spectator in dramatic theatre because there is no way out for the hero is entirely apposite to the situation of Riccardo in the last act. The fact that there is no escape for him is not so much due to the historical circumstances obtaining at the time against which he has been campaigning and which, in Brechtian terms, ought to be susceptible of change, but to the nature of the character of Riccardo himself and his convictions. Only one thing drove him to go to Auschwitz : his faith, which demands that he should act in accordance with his moral principles even under circumstances which will result in his own destruction, and it is this unconditional bond with a higher principle which renders Riccardo a truly tragic figure in the classical sense of the term.

The principle itself is spelled out in Act 3, Scene 2 when Riccardo informs the abbot of his resolve: 'It is not a question of Auschwitz any more. —The idea of the papacy must be kept pure for all time.' (II,122) In every word of that second sentence can be heard a reflection of the unshakeable and transcendental quality of his principles which gives meaning to his actions in the face of the horrifying realities of Auschwitz. The essential purpose of the fifth act is to highlight this conflict between principle and reality. The political message of the play, which is broadly put across in 'epic' terms, is over and done with in the fourth act, where the scene with the Pope takes place. If we add to this Hochhuth's proposed alternative ending, the reworked version of Act 3, Scene 3, that would suffice to place before the spectator once more the consequences for the Jews in general and Riccardo in particular. But, as the epithet 'Christian tragedy' indicates, the author is concerned to permit his hero to score a moral victory. And this is why the fifth act takes the dramatic conflict on the tragic plane to its ultimate conclusion.

The internal dramatic conflict is elevated in this final act into the realm of Christian faith. This is the real reason behind the introduction of the doctor, who also has one actor reserved to play his part and no other. The Auschwitz doctor is no straightforward Nazi. He is explicitly conceived as a satanic figure, the dramatic personification of the evil principle. In a stage direction about the doctor, Hochhuth writes that his introduction serves the purpose of 'at least hinting at the possibility that in the doctor an ageless figure of the theatre and of Christian mystery plays has once more made his

entrance'. (II,28) The doctor too has a model in real life
drawn from historical accounts of Auschwitz. And the
writer Gerhard Zwerenz has good cause to call the
closing scenes, in which the doctor appears, 'Dantesque,
and all the more so because, sadly, they are so absolutely
true to reality'.[29]

In both word and action, the satanic doctor emerges
as an appropriate counter figure to Riccardo, the
Christian hero. The doctor states with confident scorn :

> In truth : creator, creation, and created
> are all refuted by Auschwitz.
> Life as an idea is dead. (II,194)

When Riccardo contradicts this, he is set to work in the
crematorium. And in the scene that follows the priest
confesses to Gerstein, who is seeking to free him from
Auschwitz, that in working there his faith really has
begun to falter :

> It was an act of presumption to come here.
> I cannot hold on, truly I cannot.
> . . .
> With every human being that I burn
> A piece of my faith burns.
> God burns.
> . . .
> If I knew that—He were looking on,
> (with repugnance) I should have to hate Him.
>
> (II,211)

This does not, however, mean that there is any basis for
Holthusen's objection that Riccardo has been drawn in
such a way that as a martyr he has 'no real weight', and
that the doctor drives him 'to the wall'.[30] The dialogue
at this juncture makes it clear that he is indeed at the

end of his psychological tether, but his moral resolve stands unshaken, founded as it is on faith in an ideal :

> I atone, I must do it.
>
> . . .
>
> I represent the Church.
> I may not go, whether I want to or no.
> And God knows I have wanted to go. (II,212)

The more he is exposed to temptation, the greater his steadfastness becomes. The last words he addresses to the doctor call back to mind the conviction which he expressed in the previous scene, that paradoxically the satanic figure of the doctor confirms the existence of God. Then he hurled these words at the doctor :

> Your face filled with lust and filth and idiocy . . .
> drives every doubt away—every single one. Since
> the devil exists, God exists too :
> otherwise you would have conquered long ago.
>
> (II,197–98)

Now he assures him calmly : 'You will never bring off the victory, that is why you are so voluble. Your kind only have fleeting triumphs.' (II,217) He even tries to shoot the doctor, but in the attempt he is himself shot down by an SS guard. Riccardo's dying words are in the form of a prayer, which once again serves to illustrate the fact that, although evil may have triumphed on the plane of earthly existence, the true victory of which he speaks is a spiritual conquest such as he himself achieves in the very moment of death.

For all its stylistic imbalances, its inordinate length, which makes the work unplayable in an uncut form, and, to be honest, some tedious passages, *The Representative* is in its original five-act version a significant and powerful drama. More than once critics have drawn

attention to the fact that its weaknesses are very similar
to those of Schiller's *Don Carlos*. The polemicism of the
main body of the drama is closely related to Brechtian
theatre, as has been shown in some detail by Zimmermann.[31] But the concluding tragic act demonstrates,
despite all the criticism levelled at it from ecclesiastical
quarters, that the play is not solely concerned with
criticising the person of the Pope and the Church which
he represents. On the contrary, as Provost Grüber once
said during a public discussion, the play as a whole poses
a different question, namely : 'Why have we all—not
just the Pope—failed as Christians?'[32] And, he continued,
the last act of the drama offers a reply to this question :
'Because the unswerving and unflinching moral conscious-
ness such as is embodied in the person of Riccardo,
represents in reality an exception, even among Christians.'
All this must of course be considered in the light of
Hochhuth's conviction that the committed individual,
and he alone, is in a position to bring about significant
change. The structure and form of the drama are such
that the issue is put and the answer presented in a
thoroughly convincing manner. And this is surely the
reason why *The Representative* has had such a unique
impact, one which has been felt far beyond the confines
of the theatre itself.

IV

SOLDIERS

Hochhuth's second drama, *Soldiers*, subtitled 'Obituary
for Geneva', is once again called a tragedy by its author,

epic

although there is, as before, a strong admixture of epic elements. In the years 1964–1966, during which Hochhuth was working on the play, the 'documentary theatre' was at its height: Kipphardt's Oppenheim play appeared, as did his *Joel Brand*; Peter Brook's Vietnam play *US* appeared; and Peter Weiss's *The Inquiry* was staged—he was still working on his *Vietnam Discourse* (*Vietnam-Diskurs*) in 1967. Once more documentary material forms the basis of Hochhuth's drama. And, once more, the subject matter is extremely sensitive politically; this time especially in England, where the play is set. It was to have been produced in London by the National Theatre, but it was banned; only after the abolition of theatre censorship in Britain was it possible to perform it, and the book edition of the play was long delayed.

The documents Hochhuth used in the making of *Soldiers* cover two subjects: the Allied war in the air against Nazi Germany, and the mysterious circumstances surrounding the plane crash which cost the life of General Sikorsky, Prime Minister of the Polish government in exile, off Gibraltar in July 1943. According to the play, Churchill was instrumental in bringing about the crash for reasons of state. Hochhuth found an important champion of this viewpoint in the historian David Irving.[33] Hochhuth, however, does not regard *Soldiers* as documentary theatre any more than he did his first play, but rather as historical drama. The central figure of Churchill is deliberately shown in situations which are mostly the product of Hochhuth's imagination. But in so doing, he has with typical thoroughness made a study of the political circumstances relating to the play as well as of the habits and idiosyncracies of his chief protagonist. The amusing dream-tale *L'Impromptu de Madame Tussaud*, which was discussed earlier,

hist drama

Ch

affords some insight into the way in which his attention was completely taken up with the drama during its composition.

Soldiers has a framework, which gives the central part of the action—the 'play within the play'—a very theatrical flavour and underlines the fact that the work is essentially 'epic' in intent. And, as in *The Representative*, the verse form is employed to avoid any temptation to slip into heavy-handed realism. Although it is 'epic', the central part of the play is very un-Brechtian—it is only epic in the sense that every historical drama is, namely, in relation to the links with historical reality beyond the immediate context of the action. These links are indeed highlighted by Hochhuth in his detailed notes accompanying the dialogue. Hochhuth the self-confessed 'servant of history' is extremely meticulous in this respect, and with the themes he has chosen he certainly has to be; factual accuracy is essential, as Siegfried Melchinger writes, because the truth or otherwise of the material can readily be verified. Not only that : 'It is . . . doubly indispensable when the truth does not lie on the surface, but has to be rooted out, uncovered, unmasked.'[34] This is a factor which has to be taken into account if we are to do proper justice to Hochhuth's conception of historical drama. A critic who would accuse the author of *Soldiers* of not knowing 'what he is about' because on the one hand he did not employ 'photographic accuracy in his portrayal of historical figures and events', yet on the other crammed the notes accompanying the text with 'a whole host of detail'[35] from published memoirs, fails to comprehend the true nature of Hochhuth's approach to history.

In the first place, the detailed notes and explanatory material serve the very necessary function of supporting his controversial interpretation of an historical situation.

They form the basis of a three-act play which unfolds as an historical drama in the Aristotelian sense; that is, the principle of accuracy in portrayal—which Hochhuth regards as an unattainable ideal—is subordinated to the demands of dramatic tension growing out of the conflicts between the characters on stage.

The paradox which lies at the root of Hochhuth's conception of the drama derives from his understanding of the 'task of drama' in terms of an insistence on the fact 'that man is a responsible creature', (III,319) but in a non-Brechtian sense and with specific reference to a given historical situation, which often appears in a totally new light. Time and again with Hochhuth, alienation yields place to a moral evaluation of his characters. This is more or less inevitable when he presents us with a tragic, Sisyphean figure driven time and again by moral considerations to seek to attain the impossible. As a result, the spectator must needs identify with this figure on an emotional level, because a detached, critical analysis of the situation, if depicted in 'epic' terms, would lead inevitably to despair. This is the source both of the dramatic power of Hochhuth's plays and also of their disconcerting inner contradictions: the spectator is constantly having to switch from being a detached observer of an 'epic' theatre to dramatic identification and back again.

Soldiers is set in its historical context by the framework of the play, which is concerned with the 'Obituary for Geneva' of the work's subtitle. It is, of course, true that the outrage which *Soldiers* sparked off, especially in England, was mainly directed at the treatment of the Sikorsky theme and the part Churchill played in the affair. And, despite all the circumstantial evidence Hochhuth has provided, there is no conclusive proof that Churchill was implicated in the Sikorsky crash; according

to Hochhuth, the evidence does exist in a document,
copies of which are to remain locked away in the safe
deposits of three West European banks for fifty years,
out of consideration for people who were involved in the
affair and are still alive. But the other theme is no less
important : namely, the bombardment of German cities
by the English air force. And it was this theme which
made the play so topical in 1967, the year of its first
performance, because of the American bombing in
Vietnam.

The subject had been preoccupying Hochhuth for
some considerable time. At Christmas 1964, he penned
a letter to Heinrich Lübke, the then President of the
Federal Republic,[36] in which he advocated an international Red Cross law on war in the air. In his letter,
Hochhuth urges the President,

> as a patron of the Red Cross, to take up the issue
> publicly himself . . . and ensure that the long overdue
> law for the protection of civilians—and pilots—in a
> bombing war gets on to the international statute books.
> (I,109)

According to Hochhuth, Lübke

> reacted like the Berlin nuncio of Pius XII, who,
> having been directly approached to help rescue the
> Jews, declared that the matter was outside his compe-
> tence. I might just as well have written a message in
> a bottle.[37]

So, six years later, Hochhuth sent a similar letter 'once
again to the Bonn President's office in which the previous
one had disappeared in 1964', (I,107) this time addressed
to President Heinemann, once more without eliciting a
response. And he repeated the plea on the occasion of

a Vietnam demonstration in St Paul's church in Frankfurt in 1970 in his 'Appeal to Defence Minister Schmidt'. (III,327–34) Yet again there was no reply. In 1967 the American bombing war in the south against North Vietnam, in which the civilian population was bearing the brunt of the attack, had long been at its height, and it was this that gave the air war theme of *Soldiers* its topicality.

The framework of the play introduces this theme. The English theatre director Dorland, a former bomber pilot, now suffering from an incurable disease, is producing the 'play within the play' about Churchill. In the introductory scene, there is a debate about the problems of historical theatre and also about the subject of war in the air. Dorland's own son is a flying officer in the RAF, and the motive for the whole performance, which is taking place in the ruins of Coventry cathedral—which had been flattened by Nazi bombs—is the centenary of the Red Cross in 1964. Dorland, who acts as Hochhuth's mouthpiece, is using his play to lend support to an attempt on the part of the Red Cross to establish a law relating to war in the air. In this context, the framework involves various guests of the Red Cross : officers from both east and west, who are united in the resolve to make the Red Cross direct its efforts towards adapting itself to modern military strategy rather than towards dismantling it, and also a Japanese professor crippled by the atom bomb in Nagasaki. Dorland himself is still haunted by nightmares of those who were slaughtered in the bombing war.

So the principal theme of *Soldiers* is already outlined before the play proper begins. It is Dorland's intention to make it into a kind of modern 'Everyman', a 'little theatre of the world'. This is underlined by the quotation from Joseph Conrad which heads the book edition : 'The

earth is a temple, in which a mystery play is enacted . . . .'
(II,293) And Hochhuth stresses the point in a note :

> Everyman no longer fills his mind with thoughts of
> 'fleshly lustes and his treasure', unlike the Everyman
> of the 1529 play, instead he has become a soldier. . . .
> For, in an age of general conscription and of bombs
> and rockets which fall mainly on the defenceless, a
> man's conscience is exposed to its most extreme test
> during his time as a soldier. (II,296)

The play is mainly concerned with this idea of Everyman : virtually every character depicts him in one of his
aspects. This is also true of the figure of Dorland in the
framework, one of the 'exemplary sinners of the age',
(II,296) who seeks to atone for his involvement in the
bombing war by putting on the play within the play.
But the most important embodiment of Everyman is the
central character, the political virtuoso Churchill, who
suffers no remorse for his actions.

As the drama demonstrates, Churchill is a soldier like
his subordinates, although it is true that he is a unique
figure in an unprecedented situation. He stands at the
centre of each of the three acts which form the main
body of the drama. Both of the principal themes are
explored in their relation to Churchill. Operation
Gomorrah, the subject of Churchill's opening words,
concerns the planning and execution of the total oblitera-
tion of a German city in 1943 (the chosen target being
Hamburg). The second theme is that of the 'necessary'
elimination of an ally and friend for the sake of political
considerations. The Polish Prime Minister in exile,
General Sikorsky, threatens to sow discord among the
allies with his demands on behalf of Poland and his
hostility towards Stalin. The latter insists on his removal.
The play shows how Churchill, with the utmost

reluctance, resolves to arrange for the fatal crash to take place.

Both themes are developed in parallel throughout the course of the three acts. The Gomorrah plan is first discussed at the beginning of Act I, when one of the key figures in the scheme, the professor of physics Lord Cherwell, explains the technical conditions necessary for setting off a fire storm, with which he hopes to obliterate the target city. In the second act, photographs of Operation Gomorrah are handed round, and these show that it has been a complete success : Hamburg has been totally flattened. The centrepiece of the third act is the great debate between Churchill and Bell, Bishop of Chichester. Bell's plea to Churchill to put an end to area bombing of residential districts falls on deaf ears, since Churchill is convinced that it will materially shorten the war.

The other theme, that of Sikorsky, is interwoven with that of the war in the air. At the end of the first act, Sikorsky makes a personal attempt to engage Churchill's sympathies on behalf of the Polish people. This argument, which is just as embittered as the dispute with Bishop Bell, shows us that the general is fighting a battle that has long since been lost. He insists on an investigation of the graves in Katyn, in which the bodies of Polish officers shot by Stalin had been found, and also on an undertaking that the frontier between Russia and Poland will only be discussed after the victory over Hitler. Both demands are entirely unacceptable to Churchill. But Sikorsky refuses to knuckle under : 'It may well be true— that I have been beaten. / But since it is not justly so, I shall fight on.' (II,375) With these words, he is pronouncing his own death sentence, and he knows it :

   At last this cavalryman realises that he and his people are condemned for all time to fight tanks on horse-

back. All that still keeps his morale alive is the con-
soling certainty that he himself will fall in this battle
whose outcome has been decided before it has begun.
(II,376)

The second act ends with the plan to bring about the
crash of Sikorsky's aircraft. And here again Cherwell is
involved, together with Churchill. The third act brings
the news of Sikorsky's death, which even the Prime
Minister is unable to face with imperturbability.

The two themes are not presented in a 'dramatic'
fashion, in the sense that the course of the action is
conditioned by internal dramatic developments. All that
we see is a key politician going about his daily routine
in wartime : how, for the sake of the overriding objective
—the defeat of Hitler—decisions are taken which cost
the lives of others. According to Hochhuth, this is the
only practical way of showing war in the theatre, 'to set
up the stage in the place where the directors of the war
happen to be located'. (II,415) It is an approach squarely
in the tradition of historical drama as embodied in
Shakespeare's histories, Goethe's *Egmont*, Schiller's
Wallenstein, Büchner's *Danton's Death* and many other
dramas, in German literature notably those by Grill-
parzer, Grabbe and Hebbel. Each of these dramas
focuses attention on the principals, the makers of history,
not their victims—in contrast to, say, Brecht's *Mother
Courage*.

The depiction of the growing love between Helen, the
Prime Minister's female orderly, and Lieutenant Kocjan,
a Polish partisan, forms an integral part of the action
of *Soldiers*. Indeed, the play itself begins and ends with
key exchanges between the two, and once again this
highlights the problem of dramatic unity which Hochhuth's dramas are for ever posing. The relationship

between Helen and Kocjan, which is cut from most
productions, is central to the play, since their love represents a feature internal to the action of the drama, and
one which excites sympathy and anger against Churchill's
actions. The development of the Sikorsky theme in particular has a crucial impact on this relationship. On the
last day of his stay, just before he is due to fly off for a
mission behind the German lines in Poland, Kocjan and
Helen are due to meet for one last time. In a stage
direction at the beginning of the third act, Hochhuth
reminds us of his concept of the significance of love as
the 'last unproblematical thing when it is not the psychiatrist who waits by the bedside, but death'. (II,420) But
the death of Sikorsky completely shatters Kocjan and at
the same time arouses his suspicions—he and Helen
violently disagree, and as a result their chance of being
together one last time is destroyed by the war machine
in which they are both involved. Hochhuth was not
entirely successful in blending this touching love affair
between two secondary characters and the broader
historical perspective. However, the more general tragedy
is reflected, if somewhat dully, in the meaningless prevention of an experience of love which cannot be recap-
tured, for Kocjan too is going to his death.

   Soldiers is essentially not a tragedy of specific named
individuals, but is rather concerned with mankind at
large, with Everyman in all his aspects, whether as
a maker of history, like Churchill and his aides, or as
one of those on the receiving end. The relationship
between Helen and Kocjan should, therefore, not be
regarded as a digression. As we have already seen in
The Representative, Hochhuth does not fight shy of
incorporating a personal issue like self-sacrifice into   a
wider historical drama depicting the makers of history.

   One aspect of this dual tragedy concerns the bombing

war against the German civilian population. The problem is introduced at the very beginning of the framework action, when Dorland calls to mind the sight of Dresden in flames. In addition, 'death' appears on the stage, in the shape of projections of the image of a female skull mummified in the Dresden fire storm. Again and again in the course of the subsequent action, the horrifying consequences of this kind of war are described, starting with Cherwell's terrible instructions for initiating a fire storm. The culminating point of this aspect of the tragedy is Bishop Bell's urgent appeal to Churchill to bring about a halt to area bombing. But even before the interview, it is clear that Churchill is not going to countenance the idea. His interpretation of the conditions currently prevailing will not permit him to do so, for he still believes that he can actually save human lives and shorten the war by means of these air raids.

The position of the Prime Minister is equally inflexible with regard to the other aspect of the tragedy, the Sikorsky theme. Each of the three acts ends with this theme. Here, it is true, Churchill is shown in a less optimistic vein, but this does not stand in the way of his inflexible determination to take the sole option—as he sees it—that is open to him. And in so doing, humanitarian considerations have no place for him :

Faith, tears, actions—before the demons in the power
  arena
it all collapses like
the law under an outburst of laughter. (II,376)

The essential nature of the tragedy in this situation is that, for those caught up in it, there appears to be no other path to follow, even when they are acting wrongly. This inevitable doom which hangs over the characters is also expressed in the atmosphere created in the closing

seconds of the first act; after Sikorsky has left and
Churchill remains alone on the stage, the direction reads :
'The fighter squadron rushes on, very low, very loud,
over the water, which has turned black under a black
horizon.' (II,376)

Many critics of *Soldiers* fail to recognise this aspect
of the drama; Stanley Kaufmann, for example, writing
of the New York première, considers that Hochhuth's
revelation of Churchill's possible complicity in Sikorsky's
murder loses all its impact for the very reason that
Churchill really did have no other course of action open
to him.[38] But, in contrast to *The Representative*, this side
of the argument is not the central issue. Unmasking the
facts of the situation is only of secondary importance.
Unlike the situation with Pope Pius XII, neither Churchill
nor the rest of those involved are primarily figures whose
moral failings Hochhuth is seeking to pillory. Accordingly—and again in contrast to the Pope in *The
Representative*—these characters appear before us as
'human beings'. Even Cherwell, who sets in train the
plot against Sikorsky, is forced to struggle with his own
emotions when the subject is discussed at the end of the
second act. (II,414) And when the news of Sikorsky's
death comes in, Churchill himself is visibly shaken : he
'blinks and his eyes are filled with tears', (II,445) and
he is not capable of immediate speech.

Churchill is unmoved by the sight of photographs of
'Gomorrah'—he is too much of a soldier for that—but
when, at the same time, he is told that his black swan
has been lacerated by a fox, his face becomes 'contorted';
for him it is 'good, that rage can dissolve into tears'.
(II,403) His weaknesses, then, are not concealed. As
Helen declares—and she should know—'Mr Churchill is
exclusively concerned with Mr Churchill'. (II,422) And
even the fact that the decision to continue area bombing

is itself based on a false assessment of the military situation is made explicit in the dispute with Bishop Bell, in the course of which a certain degree of superstition on Churchill's part becomes evident, but these weaknesses are never allowed to come to the fore. Time and again, Churchill's extraordinary qualities are stressed by other characters in the play. As Dorland says to Bell in Act 3 : 'If you attack Churchill, just think / where we all should be without this man.' The bishop replies : 'It is because I know that, that I am still trying / to speak with him.' (II,349) For all that, Hochhuth never lets us forget that even the Prime Minister is first and foremost a soldier, whose business is war and whose actions inevitably destroy men's hopes and lives. In this regard, he must be consistent and confident of victory; in Churchill's own words, 'That man is a soldier whom no doubts can weaken.' (II,427) But it is Bishop Bell who poses the fundamental question : 'Is a bomber pilot who deliberately destroys residential areas / still to be spoken of as a soldier?' (II,431)

In the prologue reference is made to the tendency of the soldier to disassociate himself from any form of personal responsibility when he is following his profession : 'They put on their uniforms in order to stop being individuals, to mark themselves off from those who are personally responsible.' (II,327) Churchill's personal tragedy, if he has one, lies in the fact that, for him, there is no escaping responsibility. As one who is creating history by his actions, he is also to some extent exemplary for those who have no freedom to make up their own minds, yet who, according to Hochhuth, ought to be held responsible for their actions.

Thus it is that Churchill bears some resemblance to a tragic figure, not because he comes to grief, but rather by virtue of his greatness. Because of the manner in which his character is drawn, Hochhuth constantly keeps Churchill's greatness before our eyes, and on more than one occasion seeks to transform him into a mythical figure. This is achieved not least by the settings of the play within the play—the individual acts are entitled 'The Ship', 'The Bed', and 'The Park' respectively—and these names assume the significance of symbols from the realms of the imagination. The park, for example, has strong associations with the Garden of Eden.

In the middle of the play, a stage direction stresses that these mythical elements should be made apparent in the production :

> The Prime Minister has entered from his bath naked and dripping and storm-swift as Neptune rising from the waves. The ... bath towel may indeed be draped over his sea-godlike nakedness—but not so as to degenerate into the petty documentary naturalism of statues of Churchill. ... This is the moment in the play when the author can do no more, the actor can do everything to bridge the gap between theatre and myth. ... Magic has to be present—if the actor can summon it up ... then his performance will achieve in retrospect what Churchill himself achieved. (II,410)

And Hochhuth makes this even more explicit later in the same stage direction :

> Churchill is the element itself, the personification of the drive for war, the bloodstream of that century in which more people have been violently done to death than ever before since the beginning of the world. (II,410)

This approach to the portrayal of Churchill also lends a measure of real greatness to his implication in guilt;

especially so since his guilt is the consequence of the
historical necessity—which Hochhuth has never denied—
of bringing Hitler to his knees. But, even here, Hochhuth
by no means slackens in his moral demands, as is clearly
demonstrated, for example, in the passionate appeal
which Bishop Bell directs at Churchill. Yet, at the end
of the day, the figure of Churchill stands above all
criticism. The argument of *Soldiers* is not that Churchill
ought to have acted differently, but rather that there
should be an end to this kind of approach to the conduct
of war.

In presenting us with an historical drama, an Everyman play on the tragedy of war, and with a 'hero' who
is not a tragic figure in the strict sense of the term,
Hochhuth is once again seeking to achieve a great deal
all at once. It is hardly likely that any one production of
this complex play could paper over the cracks that
certainly exist in it, although, on the whole, *Soldiers*
gives the impression of being more unified than *The
Representative*. Its greatest weakness is a certain measure
of tediousness generated by the extensiveness of the
material employed and a degree of *longueur* in the argu-
mentation. As is frequently the case with Hochhuth,
these blemishes threaten to block the progress of the
action on occasion. But he himself is aware of this problem, and draws attention to the fact in the dream tale
L'Impromptu de Madame Tussaud. (III,75) In addition,
he has followed the same practice as in other plays by
bracketing off certain sections to indicate where possible
cuts might be made.

It is a matter for regret that the majority of producers
have not taken the slightest notice of Hochhuth's wishes.
In their endeavours to mould his works to fit their own
preconceived notions, they have not infrequently muti-
lated key passages in the text. By cutting the love affair

between Helen and Kocjan, for example, which has been done in several productions, the play is certainly abbreviated, but not without doing violence to its essential nature.

Alongside the historical figures in the Everyman theatre of the world, there are other, secondary characters with whom the spectator can identify. No less important is the framework which specifically sets the action within the context of the centenary of the Red Cross in Geneva and which turns the play into the obituary it is intended to be, a funeral oration on the lost opportunities of humanity. Perhaps Hochhuth tries to do more in *Soldiers* than can be done in the theatre. The way in which he makes this attempt leaves the spectator dissatisfied in many respects, but the play does at least confront him with a central issue of our time which has long been hidden in a cloak of silence.

V

GUERILLAS

Hochhuth began work in earnest on his third play *Guerillas* in 1968, a year of unrest and protest in West Germany and many other countries, especially the USA : the American involvement in Vietnam was at its peak; and back home there was a succession of large-scale demonstrations against the war, as well as for civil rights for the American blacks. More and more members of the militant black organisation the Black Panthers were either arrested by the police or shot down; the black pastor Martin Luther King and Senator Robert Kennedy both met their death at the hand of an assassin; and Richard Nixon was eventually elected to the White House in the November of that year. The same year saw in Czechoslovakia the blossoming of the 'Prague Spring' under Alexander Dubcek, and his subsequent overthrow when the Russian invasion came; in Brazil, the Commission of Human Rights was investigating the systematic genocide of the Indian population; a few months previously in Bolivia, the Argentinian revolutionary Che Guevara had been taken prisoner and put to death.

In West Germany, the Grand Coalition held the reins of power under Chancellor Kiesinger; on the streets the so-called APO, the extra-parliamentary opposition, was forming up against it. The shooting of the student Benno Ohnesorg in Berlin by the police during a demonstration against the Shah's visit had happened only a few months previously (on 2 June 1967); and in April an attempt on the life of the student leader Rudi Dutschke sparked off the Easter riots. In May came the students' and workers' riots in France.

All these events are reflected in *Guerillas*. Hochhuth takes his stand somewhere between the opposing parties. For him, no other path was possible : he had already made this clear in the course of a public debate on 'Strengths and weaknesses of the political theatre' which took place before a thousand or so students in the Free University of Berlin, and he subsequently put his views down on paper in an article for the journal *Konkret* on 18 September 1969. For all his opposition to the policies of the Federal government and the United States administration, Hochhuth is clearly far from being a sympathiser of the APO and the student supporters of Rudi Dutschke.[39] Objections were raised against *Soldiers* on the grounds that it did not portray the social factors which led to the war being conducted in a manner which he condemns; but Hochhuth has no faith in the utopian vision of Herbert Marcuse, and he certainly regards protests and demonstrations as no way to achieve positive objectives. The decisive factor which led to the composition of *Guerillas*—'the key experience which left its stamp on the political thesis of my *Guerillas* play'—was, as Hochhuth wrote later, an anti-Vietnam demonstration on May Day, 1968, in New York :

> We were treated by the New York police, one might almost say 'mothered' by them, in such a way that I said at the time that demonstrations sanctioned by the police should be banned by their organisers. It was a thoroughly humiliating and farcical experience; and if anyone had the least suspicion that that society might be overthrown on the streets, or by demonstrations on University campuses, this demonstration would have put an end to it. . . . The only purpose it served was to bear witness to the utter political impotence of the demonstrators.[40]

The recipe for social change which Hochhuth proposes instead is what he calls revolution by infiltration. This is spelled out in his essay 'About *Guerillas*: No Revolution without Infiltration', (I,217–46) and is discussed in relation to the United States in 'Fear of the protective power USA', the first version of which appeared in *Konkret* in 1968. The play itself represents the practical application of his theory in dramatic terms.

The principal figure, around whom the action revolves, is an American Senator by the name of Nicolson. He organises and heads a conspiracy, the object of which is to seize an atomic submarine and take hostages with the object of forcing a change in the power structure of the United States to the benefit of the population as a whole. The individual scenes show the various plans and

preparations being made by members of the establishment who have joined the plot, and in them all the
problems attendant upon such an undertaking are discussed, not least the necessity for retaining secrecy and
excluding potential traitors to the cause and also the
unavoidable issue of blood-letting.

In the course of his work, Nicolson has been dealing
with CIA officials; and they too have to be kept in
ignorance of the truth. An additional complication is
the revolutionary struggle in South America, in which
the Senator is also involved. This further burden is too
much for him, and puts his work in the United States at
risk. His wife, who comes from South America, assists
him in his activities there. She is unmasked by the CIA
and murdered; as a consequence, Nicolson's own involvement in South America is discovered; and so, in
order not to prejudice the revolutionary plans in the
north as well, Nicolson finally concurs in his own murder
by CIA colleagues, which is to be dressed up as suicide.
At the close of the play, his successor lives on,
undiscovered.

Guerillas has been subjected to the same well-aired
objections from the critics as Hochhuth's other works
for the theatre. Georg Hensel, writing about the Stutt-
gart première in May 1970, complains :

> There are . . . hardly any dramatic situations, only
> characters gathered together in groups suitable for
> discussions to take place, spiced with secret service
> cloak and dagger stuff. Hochhuth's play is no drama,
> nor yet a tragedy; it is a polemic with badly organised
> arguments.[41]

It is all too easy to raise objections of this nature, which
assume that there is somewhere a model for the drama,
according to which a play must be filled with action and

sparing with talk or polemics. Such an attitude fails to take account of the fact that in reality there is a convention of the 'conversation piece' or 'society drama' in modern theatre, which has produced a string of plays from TS Eliot to John Osborne consisting primarily of discussion, or even chit-chat. Significantly, Hochhuth himself says of the first performance of *Guerillas* in Vienna, where the producer refrained from employing alienating devices such as slide or cine projection, speakers reading out news reports, and the like :

> In Vienna the play was performed as a kind of American 'society drama'. The producer did not try to provide the audience with additional information on the facts given to them by the dialogue itself. And in my view that was the most successful production of *Guerillas* there has been.[42]

Nor does Hensel's objection about 'secret service cloak and dagger stuff' begin to hold water, since it is those very parts of the action that sound incredible which are based on fact. One such example is the scene 'Prison Visit', (II,528) in the course of which two men succeed in forcing a prisoner serving a life sentence to agree to 'confess' to the murder of Martin Luther King, after his escape from prison has been engineered. In exchange, he is offered the prospect of months of pleasure and freedom before his death. The prisoner's prompt admission of responsibility for the murder will prevent the case from being subjected to a thorough investigation. There are several such scenes in *Guerillas* which are 'dramatic' in every sense of the word, for example, the 'elegant' murder of a diver who has been spying on members of the conspiracy, (II,615–17) and the opening scene of the fifth act, in which Nicolson's wife Maria is abducted by CIA agents. (II,664)

To accuse Hochhuth of indulging in cheap sensationalism is to fail to recognise the realities of contemporary life, as other critics have conceded, Hellmuth Karasek among them.[43] Acts of assassination or abductions, not only of political opponents, but also of diplomats and others, were commonplace even in 1970, especially in South America. Since that time, facts have come to light about the activities of the CIA which more than justify Hochhuth's dramatic inventions. A book written by former CIA officials, *The CIA and the Cult of Intelligence* (1974),[44] tells us, for example, that one important wing of the American secret service really was exclusively concerned with organising such activities. This highly specialised division of the CIA, which had vast sums of money at its disposal, went under the name of Clandestine Services. According to the book, it paid agents who operated for them in the greatest secrecy. The authors write about the work of one such 'clandestine operator' that he frequently found himself on the fringes of the underworld, and sometimes in the thick of it. He made use of criminals, especially when something unsavoury had to be done with which he did not want to become involved directly, or when he did not want to risk the CIA becoming implicated in his own dirty work. This sort of clandestine operator, needing an attractive young woman to compromise foreign officials, did not draw on female employees of the CIA, but used local prostitutes.[45] It is hardly surprising that the CIA went out of their way to prevent the publication of this book. The facts it discloses leave one in no doubt whatever that everything which Hochhuth invented about the CIA, however far-fetched it may sound, might well have been quite commonplace in 1970.

One critic, Hensel, has voiced a third and equally typical objection to *Guerillas* :

His hotch-potch of historical authenticity and political science fiction leaves hopelessly unanswered the question of what is true and what is only either well invented or mere cloak and dagger.[46]

This kind of criticism is totally irrelevant to the judgement of this play either as literature or as theatre, since *Guerillas* is not a documentary play. It is not written first and foremost in order to convince the audience of the reality or plausibility of such happenings. In the case of this as well as of his previous plays, the reader of the book edition may well find himself irritated by Hochhuth's Shavian practice of providing extremely personal and subjective commentaries on contemporary history in his foreword and the notes accompanying the text. The audience, however, is, of course, spared these marginal observations and the drama itself is left free to stand or fall on its own merits. When views of that nature are repeated by characters in the play—for example, the assertion that the White House is ruled by a 'Mafia'— they constitute the opinions of committed guerillas, and that is the reason why they have become guerillas. Otherwise they would hardly think or talk like that.

The historical and documentary aspects of the drama are, as was the case in *Soldiers*, not an end in themselves, only the foundation on which the writer builds his theme proper, which is contained in the quotation by Goethe which Hochhuth cites in his foreword: 'What good is there at all in us if it is not the strength and the inclination to employ worldly means in the service of higher objectives?' (II,492) So once more we are dealing with a political play concerned with contemporary issues, located in an historically significant location, but one in which these elements are not the key factors. *Guerillas* is set in the United States in the years 1967–1968, im-

mediately before the assassination of Robert Kennedy
(with whom the central figure of the play has more than
a little in common), that is to say, in a closely defined
and familiar situation which at the time of the play's
première lay in the immediate past and the effects of
which were still being felt.

For all that, *Guerillas* is really an historical drama in
reverse, as it were. Hochhuth ploughs through the
'midden of documentation', not, as he stresses, in order
to reconstruct a past epoch, but to project possible happenings in the future. It is in this respect that *Guerillas*
differs from other historical plays written about the same
time—Tankred Dorst's *Toller*, for example, or the documentary theatre of Kipphardt and Weiss. Unlike these
plays, *Guerillas* does not pose the question : What actually happened? *Soldiers* was largely concerned to answer
this kind of question, whilst *The Representative* also
raised the question : What would have happened, if . . .?
(If, for example, the Pope had broken his silence.)
Guerillas, on the other hand, is explicitly concerned with
the question : What might happen in the future? It
deals with what Hochhuth regards as the one and only
possibility of bringing about revolutionary change, that
is to say, by infiltrating the existing power stucture, and
he uses the United States by way of illustration.

And that is why the argument about the logicality of
Hochhuth's political judgements, which other critics have
made so much play of, is only a side issue. Georg Günther
Eckstein, for example, is wrong when he states that

the key issue remains : Has America really . . . reached
a degree of torpor in which there is no other way out
but desperate permutations of coups d'état and guerilla
struggles? And Hochhuth's erroneous answer leaves
the play shorn of all political credibility.[47]

Hochhuth may not be presenting a true picture of the real situation in America but, given the broad facts of the situation as they are generally known, the circumstances of the members of the conspiracy in *Guerillas* are related in a convincing enough manner for them to hold together as an illustration of what might happen, and what actions should be avoided. Besides, Hochhuth is in pursuit of historical truth; this is underlined by his conception of historical drama no less than by his theoretical stance on this issue. (I,142ff)

Hochhuth is fully aware of the fact that he is of necessity placing before his audience a string of crude generalisations. He recognises that he is presenting on stage a 'theatrical' version of New York :

> What lies behind this exercise is the fact that reality of itself is always tedious, no more than raw material —it only becomes inspiring and illuminating if it is employed in the service of ideas. So this play takes as its base the current New York establishment like the shell of a building bought up for scrap, and seeks to illumine it with a revolutionary spirit which will enable us to see through its façade. In so doing, the symbolical qualities of reality have been refined from the dross; and the characters that perform on this stage are as un-naturalistic as their language—for they are the mouthpieces of ideas. (II,498)

So *Guerillas* is concerned with ideas, acted out within the context of an America which is indeed fictitious, but could form part of reality as we know it. The play discusses the question of a future which even today is not beyond the bounds of possibility.

In *Guerillas*, Hochhuth the 'epic' dramatist goes beyond Brecht in one important respect. Like Brecht, he seeks to demonstrate that our world is susceptible of change. What happens on stage is, on the one hand, rendered 'epic' in that continual direct references are made to the world of the spectator, thus alienating him from the action and preventing him from indulging in uncritical sympathy or identification with the characters on stage. But it is at this point that Hochhuth's alienation technique differs from that of Brecht. The latter, it is true, translates the action of his plays into another sphere, a fact which Hochhuth deplores in his foreword, since it is most often a fairytale realm, where the events to be shown are 'prettied up in fancy dress like the parable from Sezuan'. (II,497) In Hochhuth's eyes, this results in a dilution of the political issues, since people simply do not take such 'fairytales' seriously enough. Other writers, notably Dürrenmatt, equally alienate the action of their dramas, but they weaken their impact by transposing them into the sphere of the grotesque. The setting in which Hochhuth, by contrast, locates the action of *Guerillas* is Utopia, understood in terms of a state which does not yet exist but which can be visualised as an extrapolation of present reality.

Through the medium of a sequence of actual events on stage, the spectator is shown a conflict between the possibilities of change and the obstacles that lie in its path, in order both to enable him to recognise these obstacles more clearly and also to work out for himself the directions which these movements towards change might take.

Although *Guerillas* contains a great deal in the way of discussion on the various issues raised, there is also a developing action in the traditional sense of the term, and the central figure even incurs a measure of tragic guilt. *Guerillas* is truly a tragedy in the classical sense; not, as in the previous plays, a tragedy of Christianity or of mankind, but one which is exclusively concerned with the fall of its 'hero' and clearly reflects Hochhuth's view of the function of the individual in a political situation. Any critic conscious of trends in creative writing in recent years will find it hard to swallow the fact that, long after Naturalism, Sternheim, Brecht and the Absurd, someone is still daring to state in the theatre that, despite our technological mass society, individual responsibility is not a thing of the past, that individual action directed towards a specific objective can still achieve decisive change, and that this someone has actually exhumed tragedy, which has long since been pronounced dead and buried, in order to demonstrate how an independent individual, confronting other equally responsible individuals, incurs guilt and comes to a tragic end.

Hochhuth did not of course select this form out of obtuseness or backwardness. His choice is justified by the theme itself. In his foreword, Hochhuth quotes the sociologist Max Weber :

> The real danger . . . does not lie with the masses. The core of the socio-political problem does not reside in the economic situation of the governed, but is rather related to the political qualifications of the governing classes and those climbing the social ladder. (II,500)

And, on the question of Utopia, he states that it frequently fails to be achieved, 'not because of technical or material shortcomings', but, as in the case of the Utopia projected in *Guerillas*, 'simply and solely because of an irremediable shortsightedness among contemporaries'. As Galbraith said, 'some individual or other has to take the initiative'. (II,501) And the depiction of such an individual is the true stuff for tragedy.

It is difficult indeed to refute Hochhuth's assertion that, even today, it is individuals who are feared by governments, capitalists, bureaucrats and technocrats throughout the world. This can be seen not only in the trials of intellectuals in eastern Europe but also by the assassination of key personalities in the United States like Robert Kennedy or Martin Luther King. And one such personality in *Guerillas* is the politically influential and extremely wealthy Senator Nicolson. At one point, he makes it clear that it is his vulnerability as an individual that has led him, despite all his influence, not to employ constitutional means to come to power :

> If I actually used my dollars
> to bring into being
> a Workers' Party of 300,000 members
> then I would be shot down. (II,635)

Hochhuth makes use of an historical figure to illustrate his theme of the fate of an individual involved in subversive activities, namely, Che Guevara, who in *Guerillas* hides behind the pseudonym of 'Major Adams'. What Che Guevara was for South America, Nicolson is to be for the United States, and his social status renders his chances all the more favourable. The fact that Nicolson is conceived in dramatic, even tragic terms is clearly intended to cause the spectator to identify with him on an emotional level, and this is certainly not intended to conflict with the epic elements of the play—the theoretical discussions which punctuate the action—but rather to strengthen and supplement them.

Thus it is that the Senator who heads the conspiracy combines within himself the essential features of the classical tragic hero : his individual actions are guided by moral considerations; he experiences guilt, both as a result of having to bring about the death of opponents and also because of his fateful involvement in the revolution in the south on top of his activities in the north; he permits nothing to divert his attention from his ideal objectives; he is not simply destroyed by external factors, but through a combination of his own shortcomings and chance occurrences, in which the workings of 'fate' are to be seen; and at the very moment of his fall he succeeds in scoring a moral victory, since by accepting the fact of his own death the plans for a coup d'état in the north are able to remain secret.

Despite the large cast and the wealth of factual material in *Guerillas*, the work is very carefully organised and constructed, although its division into five acts is somewhat confusing and does not do full justice to the material. In effect, there are eight principal scenes and an equal number of secondary scenes, acted on the apron stage, which alternate with one another. The latter are mainly tactical demonstrations or theoretical discussions by members of the conspiracy. Exceptions to this are 'Apron Stage II', in which a man detained by the CIA is prevailed upon to present himself as the murderer of Martin Luther King, and 'Apron Stage V', which shows a television film of a limousine with special safety features purpose-built for the American President; so both these scenes constitute commentaries on a situation in which the assassination of prominent individuals is an almost everyday occurrence.

The play can conveniently be considered as falling into three parts of more or less equal length. The introductory section takes up the three scenes of the first act (together with the subsidiary scenes). Right at the very beginning, we are introduced to the theme of the central figure's implication in guilt, that is, Nicolson and the dangerous dissipation of his energies by the additional work he has undertaken in the south, as well as the necessity for issuing assassination orders in the interests of the cause. Both themes recur many times in the course of the subsequent action. The first scene proper (Act I, Scene 1) foreshadows the closing scene of the play in many ways, (Act 5, Scene 2) both in the setting and in the characters present on stage (Nicolson, his companions and the CIA official Stryker are in the conference room of their administration building), and this lends the play a cohesive form. The first part comes to a close with the brief first and only meeting between Nicolson and Che Guevara in the guise of 'Major Adams' in Bolivia (Act 1, Scene 3). The figure of Adams is important as a leitmotif, and there are times when it almost seems as if the play really ought to have been about Che Guevara himself. In Adams's resigned words, which bring the third scene to a close, there is also an oblique reference to the subsequent death of Maria, and with it, that of Nicolson himself : 'We have come to the end. . . . The peasants are as dull as stones.' (II,569)

The central section of the play embraces the second and third acts. It commences with the long drawn-out Guevara troubles in Bolivia, and this forms the link between the revolution in South America and the north. The climactic point is Nicolson's 'Obituary for that freedom in which everyone who had reached the shores of America used to know he was cocooned'. (II,589) This is followed by the atmospherically intense and impressive leave-taking scene between the two revolutionaries. Adams/Guevara knows he is going to his death. The third act is a kind of mirror image, this time set in the north, in the United States. Here, more or less in the middle of the play, we are finally permitted to hear the ideological programme of the conspirators and their precise plans. (II,608) At the end of the scene comes the murder which the conspirators are compelled to commit against a diver who has been spying on them; and so at the conclusion of this section, we are shown not only a justification of the necessity for their actions but also a further illustration of the guilt which they inevitably incur.

The concluding section of the play centres on three key scenes: the fourth act depicts the climax of the action proper, in which the ultimate failure of the conspiracy is already projected. After a dispute between Nicolson and his conservative partner Wiener, who has seen through the conspiracy, we find out about Maria's last mission in the south and the death of Che Guevara. The two main scenes of the fifth act depict first the downfall of Maria in the south, and then of Nicolson in the north.

A close look at the structure and development of the action in *Guerillas* will readily refute the assertion that the play is neither a drama nor a tragedy. Despite its political theme, it is essentially the drama of the two protagonists Nicolson and Maria, although their fate does not actually dominate the work. *Guerillas* does not set out to demonstrate the necessity for revolution—that is taken for granted; nor is it possible to depict any conflict between opposing attitudes for as long as the conspiracy remains secret. So, with the exception of the CIA boss Stryker and his bodyguard, Hochhuth concentrates almost exclusively on the conspirators themselves.

Conflict situations proper are restricted to two areas. In the first place, we are shown a marriage at risk because it is childless. When Maria hears of her husband's plans, nothing can stand in the way of her resolve to take part herself and work for the revolution in South America. (Act 1, Scene 2) In the second place, psychological conflicts are presented—in the case of Nicolson, these are concerned with the division of his activities and also with the necessity for killing; Maria, on the other hand, has to contend not only with her conscience but also with her fears. She decides to become involved herself when she hears of the torture and murder of another woman by CIA agents. This overshadows her actions until she herself comes to a similar end. Later her problems with her conscience help her abducters, since it keeps her away from the altar of the church, where she would perhaps have remained safe a little while longer.

In the concluding scene of the play, Nicolson's end is shown to have been determined by Maria's death, since it not only shatters his mental equilibrium, but gives his opponents the necessary pretext for the assertion that he committed suicide. This scene makes it clear that the tragedy does not lie in the actions committed by the Senator and his wife, but in their personalities. Their downfall does not bring in its train the failure of the revolution they had planned. On the contrary: if Nicolson finally comes to accept his own death, it is with the intention of saving the plans for the revolution in the north, which have not yet been betrayed—now no one will be able to wring any confessions out of him. He had long since issued detailed instructions in the event of his death. The black bodyguard, Mason, has been designated as his successor. At the end of the play, he has nothing to say about Nicolson's murder, since—in the words of the stage direction—he needs 'all his powers to mask the fact that he is succeeding him'. (II,699)

So, despite Nicolson's death, 'Operation Twilight', the revolution in the north, can still be carried through. In the last part of the play, then, the personal tragedy of the hero, which engages the emotions of the spectator, plays second fiddle to the depiction of Utopia, and this is why personal fate is not given so much emphasis as in a traditional drama. Utopia represents the epic element of the drama, through which the audience is challenged to think about the world about them, and perhaps also about their own actions. The end of *Guerillas*, in true

Brechtian fashion, leaves the real issue unresolved. True, the individual who took far too much upon himself inevitably came to grief. But even if he cannot avert his fate, this does not mean that any attempt to bring about changes in the social order will necessarily be doomed to failure. The audience is left with the question as to whether the revolution which Nicolson aspired to bring about might not still break out in the near future.

But since, in the kind of society depicted in *Guerillas*, there is not the least likelihood that people at large will change their attitudes in the foreseeable future, the only obstacle, it seems, which prevents the dawning of a new age is individual inertia. Political problems of this nature, which Hochhuth implants in the minds of his audience as they leave the theatre, will certainly not inspire them to storm the barricades. But perhaps *Guerillas* represents the most that political theatre can ever hope to achieve.

VI

THE MIDWIFE

Hochhuth's first comedy, written between 1970–1971 and bearing the title *The Midwife* (*Die Hebamme*), has an appendix called : 'As an Afterword a Look at Words', (III,28ff) which provides a clear indication of the way in which the play is meant to be taken. The afterword is about the 'words of the monsters' (that is to say, the Nazis—the phrase comes from Victor Klemperer's 'Lingua Tertii Imperii'). It concludes with a list of such phrases, starting off with 'concentration camp incapacitated', and continuing via expressions such as 'meriting 'advancement' to 'symptom of moral degeneracy'. The closing lines of the afterword proper offer an explanation :

It is bad enough having to deal with a bureaucrat outside the theatre—and that is something everyone has to do every day. In the evening, we would only consider coming up against one again if we could laugh at him. But it is only as a man that he is funny, not as one who employs such words, many of which, but not all, turn him into a monster, if he isn't one already busily coining the words himself. (III,302)

The play, then, is concerned with humanity and with what words an individual uses to describe his 'human nature'.

Comedy indeed seems the appropriate medium for a subject like this, but Hochhuth's painstaking thoroughness familiar from his other dramas, which now and then strikes one as being rather pedantic, and his long, frequently moralising digressions, hardly lead one to expect that he is capable of writing in this vein. On the other hand, as Kenneth Tynan records, Hochhuth has himself confessed that 'he was always the class comedian at school and could not understand how he came to be writing tragedies'.[48] The answer to that may well lie in the nature of the subjects he chose for his previous dramas.

The critics had, of course, long since branded him as humourless, dry, moralising, and even as a 'zealot'. Many of the reviews of *The Midwife* reveal that he still tended to be regarded in this light. Hellmuth Karasek, for example, wrote in a review which can only be described as plain malicious :

Hochhuth's relationship to humour is about as close as

that between a seal and the Sahara. How on earth is
humour supposed to flourish in such an antiseptic, un-
erotic ambience, how can denunciatory zeal which
expresses itself solely in terms of dismal characterisations when it meets abuses in society expect to be
capable of such a thing as satire?[49]

Rhetorical questions of this nature tell us a great deal
about the prejudices of the critic against a dramatist but
nothing at all about the play itself.

Leaving aside Dürrenmatt's grotesque satires, it is in
fact hard to find a more convincing play written in the
Federal Republic which has sought to criticise an aspect
of contemporary society through the medium of comedy.
Even Martin Walser with his *Oak and Angora* (1962) or
Herr Krott larger than Life (*Überlebensgross Herr Krott*)
(1964) has only been partially successful; and Walser's
later comedies have not strayed outside the sphere of
private life. In *Oak and Angora*, the humour directed
against the reality of Nazism is all too often ill-placed,
and both the characters and the action of *Herr Krott*
suffer from an excess of abstraction, and this latter play
really deserves the expression 'transfer picture comedy'
which Karasek bestows on *The Midwife*. And what
other social critical writers of comedy had there been
in West Germany up until the première of *The Midwife*
in 1972? Karasek is quite wrong to assert that

Hochhuth is capable only of using blind adulation
(making his heroine about as credible as a do-gooder
in a write-up in the gutter press) or black denunciation
—instead of building up a character, he cobbles
together bits and pieces of spiteful facts about him.[50]

It hardly needs pointing out that comedy, of its very
nature, inevitably works with types, and that fully

rounded characters psychologically accurate to the last detail are quite foreign to it; but having stated that, *The Midwife* of all plays does succeed in going beyond the creation of types and cardboard characters—we are often drawn to pity the weaknesses of the very people we are laughing at on the stage, weaknesses with which the spectator sympathises, and which are understandable in the situation as it is depicted.

To return to the afterword; in it, Hochhuth quotes Goethe's dictum :

And so I have learned most clearly that language is no more than a surrogate, whether we are seeking to give expression to inner preoccupations or to external sense impressions. (III,300)

Language, then, is seen as a surrogate, as an imperfect substitute for what is actually meant. This also holds true for Hochhuth's statement that 'the Nazis invented and used words much more frequently in order to arouse fear than to disguise the facts', (III,293) and that this happened because they themselves were afraid. There is another aspect to language being used to help man maintain his psychological defences, and that is, it serves to enable him to deny his own fears, which he has suppressed into his subconscious mind, and at the same time to inspire fear in others. So it becomes a substitute for an absence of inner strength, enabling the individual to seem less weak in his own eyes than he actually is. By such means, the knowledge of his own helplessness is kept away from his conscious mind, remaining on a subconscious level. In its place, the individual constructs for himself a substitute 'self' which he can continually use to confirm his own importance, and which becomes for him an indispensable means of exercising power over others. The rôle he plays in society, the uniform he may wear, his money, which makes him into an object of envy : all these things assist him towards this end. And in the eyes of the world he secures what he has achieved by such means with the help of his 'persona', the mask he presents to the world, the purpose of which is to delude those about him into thinking that he really is as he seems to be, that he is successful when in truth he is a failure, responsible when he is really corruptible, and so forth. At this stage, he is now employing language exclusively in the service of these objectives.

The Midwife takes as its theme these substitute identities of people estranged from their true selves which they have built up artificially and which they employ language to defend with all their might. The play, then, stands foursquare in the classical comic tradition which reaches back to Molière. It pokes fun, not so much at people as such, but rather at their frantic efforts to appear more than they are in reality.

In addition to this, *The Midwife* is also concerned with a concrete social issue, the problems of the homeless in the Federal Republic, which have preoccupied Hochhuth for many years, and about which he has amassed a great deal of documentary material. He first raised the issue back in 1965 in an essay, 'The Class Struggle is not over'. In 1971 Hochhuth actually addressed a letter on the subject to the Federal Chancellor Willy Brandt, in which he puts forward specific proposals for the resolution of the problem and estimates the number of homeless at 800,000 at the very least. (I,247–49)

The camp for the homeless, which is where *The Midwife* is set, is situated in a town in Hesse called Wilhelmsthal, and known in the vernacular as the 'Chicago of the north'. The families living there, which include some hundred or so children, have long since given up any hope of ever being allocated more reasonable housing. They suffer not only from the cramped accommodation, dirty conditions and less than adequate sanitation, but are also discriminated against by the outside world; the occupants of the camp, for example, are not offered any employment. But they do have an ally in their midwife, Sister Sophie, who is also a CDU member and town councillor.[51] Her efforts to bring about improvements through official channels have, it is true, not met with success; but she has taken it upon herself to get them rehoused despite the fact that she is close to retirement, and she sets about achieving this objective with cunning and resolution.

Once again, then, Hochhuth is presenting an individual who acts resolutely in a situation in which those involved in it themselves can see no way out. As he has made clear in his preceding dramas, as well as in his theoretical writings, Hochhuth recognises that in the given circumstances such individuals do have the opportunity to take action which can result in positive changes. For this very reason he is accused by Karasek of 'failing to take due note of the force of circumstances, recognising only personal achievement or personal failure'.[52] Such an assertion is totally unjustified, as Renate Voss, dramatic adviser to the Kassel première, states in this challenge to Karasek:

The fact that here an individual man or woman is taking an initiative in a situation where no one else is prepared to act ... says a lot about the very thing which you call 'circumstances' and find lacking in *The Midwife*.... No audience is stupid enough, as you evidently think they are, to regard such actions as solutions in themselves. But they do regard them as

symptoms of a disease, whose function is to turn our
attention to the underlying sickness which people so
avidly sweep under the carpet.[53]

The play does, in fact, present a concrete set of circumstances, and also stresses that individuals should not seek
refuge in them and remain inactive, but that each should
do his part towards bringing about change. The key
factor is that anyone in the fortunate position of being
able to act in such a way as to bring about change is, in
Hochhuth's estimation, morally obligated to exploit any
opportunities that present themselves, a viewpoint we
have already seen put forward in *Guerillas*.

For the midwife, Sister Sophie, the opportunities arise
not only because she is a local councillor with party
connections, but also because of her respected position
in society, and not least because of the artfulness and
resolution with which she sets about cutting through the
tangle of red tape and finding a way round laws which
accentuate, if not perpetuate, injustices in society. It is
for this reason that, for many years now, Sophie has been
giving herself out as a Field Marshal's widow, the real
widow having died in the confusion of the immediate
post-war period. The sole purpose of her masquerade is
to enable her to give the substantial pension she receives
to the underprivileged, like those now resident in the
camp. Further, she has claimed to be eight years younger
than she really is, so as to be able to continue her socially
useful work for as long as possible, and in so doing she
is also saving the state from having to pay out her pension
as a staff sister. Now that she is feeling old and in poor
health, she has become more impatient, and has adopted
more drastic measures.

First, she assists the older inhabitants of the camp to
acquire places in a Catholic old people's home, which

she has helped to build with money belonging to the
Field Marshal's widow. Then she gets the younger
women employment as cleaners in a newly-constructed
Federal army housing estate and incites the families to
occupy it. To prevent their eviction by the state, she sets
fire to the camp and in court accepts responsibility for
her action.

By objecting that in so doing Hochhuth is simply encouraging 'the strong man or, in this case, the strong
woman' to act, Karasek is failing to recognise the central
issue raised by the play. Sophie's efforts are expressly
directed towards encouraging those deprived of their
rights to go out and secure justice for themselves. She,
more than anyone, is in the best position to do this,
because her social status and career enable her to gain an
insight into the way things really are and into the possibilities for change, neither of which the homeless in the
camp have been able to do, by virtue of their underprivileged position.

Thus it is that she succeeds in persuading a television
unit to come and film the camp, something none of its
occupants would have been able to achieve. Her plan is
thwarted by the municipal authorities, who are anxious
for their reputations; in a deliberate attempt to mislead
them, the town clerk makes the television people believe
that the camp is about to be evacuated soon anyway, and
the occupants rehoused in new accommodation nearby
—this is the housing set aside for the Federal army
personnel. But Sophie gets to know about this, and seizes
the opportunity to take the town clerk at his word. She
explains the circumstances to the occupants of the camp,
and tells them to take the initiative themselves :

> If I tell you who has frustrated
> the attempt to get the TV to show the public

> how you are suffering here—then I hope
> you will become militant—and ... act. (III,202)

The decisive factor is that Sophie, because of her social and professional advantages (not to forget her assumed status as the widow of a Field Marshal), has a wide range of possibilities for action which are not open to the less privileged members of society, especially when they happen to be living in a camp for the homeless. On top of this, such is her personality that she is able to play off the representatives of the various political parties one against the other. And, because of her age and delicate health, she does not even need to fear a prison sentence. All this means that she, in contrast to the ordinary working man or father of a family, is even able to disregard laws which may be unjust, but which for all that are still on the statute book. This she invariably does in the name of justice :

> I have never knowingly violated justice.
> But a life under German promulgators of regulations
> has taught me
> that often laws must be broken by anyone in this land
> who wants to help legality to find—true justice.
>
> (III,258)

Hochhuth is not merely seeking to point to the injustice of many laws, he is at the same time drawing our attention to the fact that the privileged in our society, whose position gives them the right kind of connections, frequently find themselves in a position to do good, if only they were able to summon up the moral courage to ride roughshod through the rule-book.

This is much truer of other figures in the play than it is of Sister Sophie. Most of them, however, exploit their position of power exclusively in order to line their own pockets. Captain Preller gives the repair contract for Federal army vehicles to the car wholesaler Koggelgritz, who pays out 300 Marks a month for the privilege, (III,117f) and who in turn has procured a cheap plot of building land for the army, presumably on the strength of his chairmanship of the local FDP. (III,115f) Schoppen, the banker, has an arrangement with the owner of a freehold farm which will ultimately secure him the ownership through mortgages which otherwise could not be transferred. On his own account he bribes Bläbberberg, the President of the Land court, in his capacity as local CDU chairman, to get the municipality to purchase the farm from him. (III,131f) And again, Gnilljeneimer, the town clerk, wants to help Koggelgritz to gain ownership of the burned-out camp for the homeless, in return for the latter's silence over the fact that the civic administration was responsible for a mishap that occurred to the local fire brigade, of which he is honorary chief. (III,325) He had had the camp barricaded in order to keep the television crew out, but this at the same time hindered the fire brigade in their attempts to put out the fire. This shows him up as a bureaucrat exploiting his position of power in an unscrupulous fashion against the interests of the occupants of the camp, simply in order to prevent himself being held up to public ridicule because of the conditions obtaining in the camp.

Sophie is the only character in *The Midwife* not to exploit her privileged position for her own ends, but rather in order to act for the benefit of the under-privileged. In this respect, she comes close to the figure of Senator Nicolson in *Guerillas*.

In *The Midwife*, the action is clearly built up 'dramatically' in the traditional sense of the term. Although Hochhuth does make use of the familiar highly detailed stage directions and notes, he remains for the

rest completely in the background. The action itself is
allowed to develop entirely on the basis of the initial
situation at the beginning of the play.

The Midwife opens with the solemn handing over of
a valuable and much sought after percussion instrument
called a crescent to the Federal army band by Baroness
Hossenbach, alias Sophie, who thereby secures the co-
operation of the soldiers in moving the old people out of
the camp, which is a precondition of her subsequent
destruction of the camp buildings. But, as has already
been pointed out, it is only the prevention of the TV
transmission about the camp by the lie told by the civic
administration that gives the homeless the excuse they
were looking for for remaining in the accommodation
they had occupied. After the fire, Sophie is hailed by the
Bild-Zeitung in true personality cult fashion as an heroic
woman helping to extinguish the flames. 'They say I put
the fires in the buildings *out*!' (III,251) she exclaims,
and in order not to be thought responsible for the exact
opposite of what she actually did, she seeks to have herself brought to trial, and it all finally ends with per-
mission being granted for the homeless to remain living
on the army housing estate. This, too, only comes about
by the underhand deal through which the army is offered
the former freehold farm in exchange. Sophie herself is
in failing health, and throughout the play she is fighting
against time, trying to realise her objectives before she
dies. And, in fact, the play closes on her death in the
courtroom.

As befits a play written in the 'dramatic' tradition, the
individual characters are more than mere mouthpieces
for ideas. Within the limitations of the comic form, they
are very realistically drawn; that is to say, they are much
more than mere cardboard figures, objects of mirth, and
even their weaknesses, at which the audience laughs, are

drawn by Hochhuth with sympathetic understanding, in accordance with his statement in the afterword that laughter is always directed at the individual, but never at one who uses the 'words of the monster', behind which the individual might be hiding himself. Anyone producing *The Midwife* is asked to ensure that criticism should be directed, not at the people, but at the circumstances that have corrupted them.

The second section of the play is preceded by a disgression on the subject of corruption in German history, which is described as being all too prevalent, and in the course of which these words are written about Captain Preller :

> He is corruptible—but for this very reason a human being, like all other family men without exception. . . . It would not be the captain but the dramatist—who earns a good deal more than Preller does—who would be comical if he got on his moral high horse about men in uniform. (III,113)

Apart from Sister Sophie, the Catholic priest Rosentreter, to whom Sophie confesses her double identity, is depicted sympathetically throughout, but so too is Judge Bläbberberg, who is involved in the corrupt dealings which were referred to earlier. His 'human' side is frequently shown, as when, for example, he defends against Pastor Bohrer a 'poor devil' whom the latter had denounced in church on grounds of onanism, (III,137) or permits a witness to quiet her baby in the courtroom, when there is nowhere else for her to go. (III,277)

Councillor Gnilljeneimer, by contrast, is by and large an unsympathetically drawn bureaucrat, one who like Bläbberberg uses the very words which are discussed in the afterword. In relation to the homeless, he says :

We live in a society where achievement counts—
and it is certain, although a matter for regret,
that there will always be a percentage of poor
    contemporaries
who by virtue of their under-achievement
are incapable of producing their social norm.

(III,161)

And yet he does manage to come to the defence of Sister Sophie, despite the fact that he wants her arrested for arson. When Bohrer voices the suspicion that she had the older members of the camp moved into the Catholic old people's home in order to deliver them up to the Catholic faith, Gnilljeneimer counters :

Why should she be concerned
to convert people to Catholicism . . .
. . .
You can do that too, father, grant the old folk
that they're got out of the camp
and put in proper housing.

(III,221-22)

But he is only shown to be capable of such human feeling when everything seems to be in accordance with the law.

Pastor Bohrer clings no less bureaucratically to a different set of rules. He is the only character in the play to be drawn as a thoroughly one-sided and importunant individual. That Hochhuth has deliberately set out to make him so is underlined by a stage direction :

Bohrer is congenitally dislikeable through no fault of his own—people like that are never right. It is a great pity, but there is nothing to be done about it; nature has already irrevocably disenfranchised him. (III,276)

Still, it is clear that injustice is done to him—no one allows him to speak when he seeks to regain the church money which Sophie has taken from his account, and so it is that he arouses a certain degree of sympathy in the audience.

The comic effect in every case derives from the audience's awareness of the disparity between the smoke-screen of morality behind which these people spend most of the time hiding and their true selves. Their sense of power and self-esteem is in the main illusory, founded as it is solely on the rôle which they play in society, as a town clerk, court or party chairman, or even as a petty bureaucrat. As people, they are the prisoners of their little fears, which they are forever trying to suppress with laughable means : through their corrupt dealings, or by having ditches thrown up in the path of the advance TV crew, or ripping the ignition cable out of someone's car to prevent him from scaring off the game in the woods. On the other side of the coin, they need their rôles as a means of self-protection; and it is only because of her rôle in society that Sophie is able to help the homeless. The upright Father Rosentreter has to assume his Jesuit mask and strain every nerve to maintain the secrecy of the confessional, in order not to betray her double identity.

The comedy is at its height in those places where the mask—the rôle behind which individuals hide—slips, and the real person is laid bare. The clearest illustration of this comes in the seventh part of the play, where Judge Bläbberberg and the Town Clerk Gnilljeneimer are wait-ing in the hospital to arrest Sophie. The medical super-intendant—acting out a superior rôle on his home ground —appears and denounces them as hooligans, and orders a policeman they had brought along to eject them for creating a nuisance. When Sister Sophie appears soon after, she has a critically ill baby in her arms. Concerned solely with performing her job, she brushes all objections aside, persuades Father Bohrer, who is also there, to carry out an emergency baptism, and has no qualms about making the two officials godparents. The turbulent scene ends with the discovery of the newspaper headline 'District Nurse fights Sea of Flames', as well as with the official confirmation that the Ministry of Defence does not want the homeless to be evicted from the housing they are occupying (the TV crew is already on the spot). So Sophie cannot be arrested, and Bläbberberg and Gnilljeneimer find themselves in a situation in which their rôles are quite useless.

The Midwife gives us an amusing and convincing picture of the false façade of social life and the inhumanity of its institutions. But no one individual is held responsible for this state of affairs : almost all the characters in the play need to conceal themselves behind the mask which their rôle affords them, and language is an essential constituent of this mask. The alienated 'language of the monsters' reduces human problems to the level of technical issues, and this makes them seem less difficult to resolve. Anyone who has this language at his command can also indulge in the illusion of a certain measure of power, and this gives him some relief for his feelings of fear and inferiority.

So *The Midwife* does far more than bring to the surface the problems of the homeless and of other underprivileged groups : it also makes a contribution to the recognition of the real nature of the society we live in, where power resides solely in whoever has the upper hand and is intent on remaining there, because the real man behind the mask is eaten away by anxiety and insecurity. Only because Sophie is not like this is she able to ride roughshod through the rules and regulations of society, and in the end she triumphs as a human being against all those who would defend unjust laws. But it is also made clear that she is very much an exception, and the nature of the social order underlines this fact.

The audience, as they laugh at a well-staged production of *The Midwife*, may well come to learn a little more about the business of acting out a rôle in our society, how much human inadequacy lies hidden behind the social mask, and at the same time how intransigent the problem is in real terms, despite the success of one resolute and privileged woman against the system.

VII

LYSISTRATA AND NATO

Hochhuth's next play was also a comedy, but this time he is dealing with a specific issue which had been preoccupying him for some years. As far back as 1964, when he wrote to the Federal President on the occasion of the centenary of the first Geneva convention (his letter was published under the title 'From Soldier to professional Criminal'; I,106ff), he alludes to the danger that the Federal Republic could find itself being used as a 'testing ground for the hydrogen bomb', (I,123) because of the fact that its allies were stationed on its territory. In his 'Appeal to Defence Minister Schmidt' in 1970, his criticism of the defence rôle of the Federal Republic as conceived by the United States is further elaborated. The appeal ends with these words:

How long will you, in the name of the Federal government, tolerate the defence policies of an ally who demonstrates ... to you in Vietnam that he under-

takes the 'defence' of friendly territory and the destruction of enemy territory with precisely the same
methods and precisely the same results! (III,334)

In the years that followed, as the war in Indo-China
continued, Hochhuth worked on his second comedy
(1971–1973). The devastation of Cambodia early in
1973 demonstrated yet again how an innocent population inevitably suffers when foreign powers are conduct-
ing a war on their territory, and how weapons of war
aimed at the enemy cause the greatest injury to the
civilian population.

In *Lysistrata and NATO* (*Lysistrate und die NATO*),[54]
which is set in the year 1967, once again, that is to say,
in the very recent past, the defoliation campaign by the
Americans in South Vietnam is brought forward as an
illustration of this threat, and presented in terms of a
television programme shown on the stage. (IV,36) A
similar fate might also befall the small Greek island
where *Lysistrata and NATO* is set, because it is ear-
marked as a NATO military base. Only united action
by all the womenfolk on the island succeeds in forestall-
ing the sale of the necessary plots of land by the peasants
to the military and thus in saving the island from their
clutches.

Once more, Hochhuth draws on a topical theme as a
starting point for the discussion of much larger issues.
The action the women take to save their island is at the
same time an act of liberation from domination by the
menfolk. Although the comedy does not, as was the case
in *The Midwife*, depend for its effect explicitly on the
gap between the way an individual presents himself to
society and the actual individual behind the mask in all
his wretchedness and weakness, here too, alongside the
amusing theme of a conspiracy of women against their

menfolk, Hochhuth is raising the same basic issues. The menfolk of the island are shown in terms of people acting out a social rôle, that of the 'man' or 'husband', in which the oppression of women is sanctioned by society. The struggle by the women, then, is inevitably more than an attempt to achieve a specific objective, it is at one and the same time a matter of principle, a fight against traditional rôle structures and sexual inequalities.

In *The Midwife*, we encountered a woman who was virtually alone in not hiding her true nature; here the women as a whole rebel against the apportioning out of rôles on the basis of sex. The rôle of 'woman' or 'wife' is essentially negative; that is to say, it serves solely to strengthen other social rôles, especially those of the man. Those who act out the rôle of 'man' can only profit from it if part of their rôle consists in oppressing those who play the rôle of 'woman'. The woman, by contrast, is defenceless, and the only means she can adopt to redress the imbalance a little is to exercise a feeling of superiority over any children she may have. The women in Hochhuth's comedy are certainly not seeking to strengthen their underdeveloped sense of self-esteem and ward off their own fears by any such contrived expedient. They have seen through the system, and by depriving those playing the rôle of 'man' of their power by the plan they adopt, they can expose the individuals hiding behind that rôle to ridicule. But, at the same time—and this is what makes the play topical—they disarm the men, and in so doing liberate not only themselves but set a precedent for the liberation of mankind at large.

As was the case with *The Midwife*, Hochhuth provides additional information about his intentions in an afterword. It is strangely moving to find here that Hochhuth, whose attitude to history had turned him into a pessimist, for the first time strikes a faint but unmistakable note of optimism. He discusses women's liberation, and the literature on the subject which had appeared in recent years. Hochhuth refers in particular to the study by Germaine Greer, *The Female Eunuch*, which first came out in English in 1970.[55] This leads him to ask whether there is a chance of making the inhuman world of men in which we all live more human, by weakening the man sufficiently to turn him into a domesticated animal :

> Only after they have exhausted their excess energy can nations or individuals be tamed, in the right frame of mind for marriage or peace-making—and this is the lesson of every age of history. And who else but women—without employing terror or force or spilling blood—would be capable of undertaking this unceasing task of weakening men—and the nations they control—in order to humanise them and of banishing aggression wherever it might exist. (IV,213–14)

This represents a logical progression from what Hochhuth wrote in his Marcuse essay in 1969, namely, that 'great powers can only be humanised when they are weakened', (II,358) and this is why he affirms the principle of international competition, which is, in his view, the only way to prevent the emergence of excessively powerful blocs. Now he applies this concept to relations between the sexes. The world of men is essentially inhuman and ridiculous because the only thing that counts in it is the artificial power of the individual's social rôle. It would, argues Hochhuth, be utterly wrong for women, as Germaine Greer also stresses, to seek to carve a niche for themselves in this kind of a world in the name of women's liberation. Given the traditional rôle of women in society, it is tempting for the individual woman to do just that.

In this context, Hochhuth quotes Otto Flake's phrase about the 'imitative nature' of women. Flake is suggesting that it is to some extent an inborn feminine attribute to copy the man and follow his ways. But this tendency, argues Hochhuth, is in fact just one further aspect of the rôle imposed upon women from birth. Passivity is the one essential quality regarded as 'feminine', apart from typical accomplishments in the home like cooking, sewing and cleaning, and, of course, motherhood. Women are not expected to be creative, either intellectually or artistically. On the contrary, they are schooled from infancy to imitate, to copy male concepts and attitudes, to fit sensitively but passively into a world dominated by men.

However, Hochhuth agrees with Germaine Greer in thinking that the time for women has perhaps now come for them to shake off this imitative proclivity and truly liberate themselves from the inhuman and destructive male world of dissimulation and oppression; at last they can once more think and feel in terms of their own proper nature, of the power of their boundless feminity, and especially their erotic power. In this context, Hochhuth refers to the discoveries of the nineteenth-century Swiss scholar Bachofen, who influenced Friedrich Engels. (IV,207ff) Bachofen was, it is true, a reactionary puritan, but in his book on the 'rights of the mother' he proved 'to the hilt' that 'the only way a woman can liberate herself from male domination is by erotic licence'. (IV,233) According to Hochhuth, the history of Europe also demonstrates quite unequivocally 'that the emancipation of women always begins with a breakthrough of erotic liberation, with the violation of "morality"'. (IV,189) By 'liberation', like 'licence', he means quite literally freeing from moral precepts, from restrictions imposed by man.

Lysistrata, the 'heroine' of Hochhuth's second comedy,

seeks to lead the way to such liberation by bringing sexual freedom to the peasant women of a small Greek island. It is modelled on the classical drama of the same name by Aristophanes. There, too, Lysistrata urges the women to refuse to yield to their menfolk until they give up their incessant warring and reconcile themselves with their enemies. Hochhuth's heroine follows in her footsteps, but this time the objective is to prevent the sale of the island to the military.

Once again, as in *The Midwife*, Hochhuth selects a 'dramatic' form in the traditional sense of the word. Hochhuth himself remains in the background, and makes no additional comments on his own account; the action is allowed to unfold entirely within the context of the internal dramatic situation and the conflicts that result between the characters. There are no signs of alienation devices, apart from the historical links with the events of the year 1967. The later version of the play, which was worked out for the Rostock production in the 1974–1975 season does, it is true, highlight the 'epic' elements more strongly; in it, the characterisations of the individual figures in the stage directions are put in the mouth of Stavros, who as it were exercises the function of a stage manager, now and again interrupting the flow of the drama and alienating it. In Rostock, too, masks were used, and this served to remove the play further from its specific context.

Lysistrata is the daughter of the innkeeper Konstantinos, who owns the sole hostelry and Turkish bath on a small Greek island. She is the only educated woman in the community, and a member of the parliament in Athens. The play is set in 1967, shortly before the Greek colonels' putsch. The funeral of two children on the island gives Lysistrata the chance to win over the other women, since the children had been struck down and killed by a caterpillar track that had broken loose from a tank during military manoeuvres. Her agitation meets with success : the wives of the more prominent peasants leave their husbands and move temporarily into the inn. Previously, Lysistrata had helped the poorer women, whose men had gone abroad to work as immigrant labour, to acquire collective ownership of the weaving mill in which they were working.

On top of this, she now encourages the women to sleep with the men from Athens who have come to investigate conditions on the island and to negotiate the sale of land with the peasants. Naturally, their action violates the laws of the world of men. It is no coincidence that these are also the laws of the Church, and this is why the local priest demands that Lysistrata should be punished and deprived of the immunity she enjoys as a member of parliament :

> For breach of the peace
> breach of the domestic peace
> for breach of marriage and family law. (IV,37)

The struggle, as has already been indicated, is not just about freeing the island but also about the general liberation of women from oppression by the world of men, and the other women on the island also see the struggle in this light. They equate the army with marriage as institutions for their suppression, and when the unmarried Lysistrata thinks the women's strike has attained its objective when the military have been beaten, one of their number tells her :

> The military, what are they
> compared to marriage !   (IV,114)

The most important male rôle on the island is played by the priest who opposes Lysistrata, since he is fully aware of the consequences of her actions. Because his wife also derives benefits from his status, she is the only woman who does not support their campaign. The peasants defend themselves as best they can. But, in the background, a more general threat from the destructive world of men is lurking, namely, the coup d'état by the Greek colonels, which is already looming on the political horizon. At the end of the play, the women do indeed succeed in saving the island, but in Athens the military have made their move. We are reminded that even a 'victory' such as hers can, given present circumstances, only be circumscribed in nature, and so Lysistrata flees to Crete.

The play has four acts, and falls into two more or less equal parts. The titles given to the first two acts —'Only a tank-track', and 'Politics—other people's money'—indicate that the first part of the play is primarily concerned with threats from the world of men. Tanks, politics and money all stand for the destructive actions of men. By contrast, the titles of the last two acts are plays on words with strong sexual connotations: 'Sword or sheath', and 'The pen(is) mightier than the sword', the last title being in English is the original. In this part, then, the emphasis is upon the women and their erotic armoury.

The second theme is, however, raised right at the beginning of the play, although in a not over-serious manner, in a sexual pantomime between Kalonika and Stavros, who are both waiters at the inn. And the act ends in a very similar fashion, although this time the game has a darker undertone : this time Kalonika takes the lead, and her antics culminate in a strip-tease, the purpose of which is to divert Stavros's attention from another lover whom she has hidden and manages to smuggle out of the room. In the second version of

Lysistrata and NATO, it is not the shepherd, but one of the peasants, which unfortunately blurs the message of the play. These two scenes apart, the exchanges between the women and their husbands are verbal in nature.

The second act depicts the world of men from a different angle. A minister living on the island, recently voted out of office, threatens to murder Lysistrata. This is a reaction on his part to her attempt to persuade him to invest the money which he has acquired through corruption in the building of a tourist hotel, in return for her silence about his underhand dealings. The minister is, however, later 'converted', even to the extent of making his feminine opponent a serious offer of marriage, which she declines. In the end, the Athenian military appear on stage, but the victory of the world of women has already been anticipated at the end of the second act, when the army fish an ancient statue of the goddess Aphrodite out of the sea. Lysistrata greets the find with enthusiasm:

> This discovery is a sign from Olympus
> as to who is to rule on the island! (IV,92)

And the stage direction adds:

> Whether or not she has read her Herodotus or has learned from more popular tradition what it is that Aphrodite demands of those who fly to her in moments of crisis seeking succour, this newly-announced 'arrival' of the goddess on this island which is under military threat is, for Lysistrata, a guarantee of her victory over the plans of the world of men. (IV,93)

Lysistrata then purloins from the army an underwater film about the retrieval of the goddess and has this film shown on television, thereby ensuring that the threatened island gets into the world press headlines.

The second part of the play shows the women in full cry. Not only do they refuse themselves to their own menfolk until such time as they agree not to sell their land, they also seduce the Athenians and arrange for their husbands to take the strangers 'by surprise'. The peasants are unable to prove that any of the married women has actually been unfaithful to her husband with one of the soldiers, but they drive them off the island none the less, never to return. Through their actions, the women have set in train the process of their eman-cipation, and they have all shared in the common initia-tive. Once more, of course, the original impetus came from a single individual who, by virtue of her privileged position, can see more than the others and has greater opportunities for action than they. But again, too, we are shown how Hochhuth regards such action on the part of an individual not, as he was accused of having done in *The Midwife*, as an open invitation to the people to shift all the responsibility on to the shoulders of the 'strong man'—or woman, as the case may be. On the contrary, Hochhuth regards it as one of the obliga-tions of such a privileged individual to show the less privileged the way towards the realisation of their own potential and to urge them to take up the cudgels on their own behalf. And this is precisely what Lysistrata does : she encourages the other women to act as a group, and they even discuss and develop Lysistrata's ideas in a body, notably her plan to drive the Athenians out by arousing the jealousy of the menfolk. (IV,121ff) There is no doubt that, in the last analysis, it is not the plotting and scheming done by a single individual which leads to the realisation of an objective, but common action which grows out of the group as a whole. This has also been demonstrated in Hochhuth's earlier plays *Guerillas* and *The Midwife*.

At the end of the great rumpus which the women cause in the fourth act, in the course of which the Athenians are driven off the island, Hochhuth presents a further symbolic representation of the women's victory over the men, not in the shape of an ancient statue, but this time a living tableau arranged in the form of a pietà. A young Athenian, wounded by the enraged peasants, cannot now depart with his comrades. Six women bear him along towards the Turkish bath, shouting out 'Let us bathe him'. This is how Hochhuth describes the scene :

> Hero Aristomenes, his head—which has more covering than any other part of his fine body—bandaged because of his wounds, is more or less carried in a sheet by Miranda (at his feet) and Sophia and Berenike—although the suspicion is strong that he is no more impaired in his limbs than he is in his masculinity. (IV,176)

A man, symbolically stripped of his rôle, and therefore weakened, is purified by a common action of the women. But Hochhuth would not be the practised dramatist he is if he did not give the scene an ironic twist in the tail : only seconds later the wife of the selfsame man, who has been the object of so much coddling, appears, having just disembarked from a ship which has put into port. She is a 'petty bourgeoise decked out in her Sunday best', spindly and looking 'like a dummy in a suburban dress-shop window, drab as forget-me-not, and thoroughly insipid'. (IV,178) Her appearance demonstrates to the spectator once again what the world of urban men and their unlimited power can do to the majority of their womenfolk; they become caricatures of women dressed up in synthetic finery, just as estranged from their own femininity and physical nature as they are from life itself. Hard on the heels of this woman, and before the spectator has ceased to laugh at her, comes the news of the colonels' putsch in Athens which brings the play to a close. (In the more recent version, this whole scene is regrettably omitted in the interests of reducing the cast numbers.)

As far as Hochhuth himself is concerned, *Lysistrata and NATO* marks a further stage along the road towards a practicable strategy for revolution, a subject which has preoccupied him since 1967 and the days of the left-wing student movement during which he was putting *Guerillas* together. Six years later, in the prefatory note to the fourth act of *Lysistrata and NATO*, he writes:

Here too we are to see how successfully women can sabotage the military schemes of men. And since revolutionary strategy demands the application of whatever weapons—short of those which might inflict physical injury or death—are most potent in the circumstances (violence is, after all, the recourse of the unimaginative male), so these women must needs fight with their bodies, whether it be by refusing them or by exploiting them. (IV,134)

Once again, the comic effect on stage of this conflict is bound up with the rôles people play. The spectator laughs especially at the helplessness of the men who appear to be men no longer when their rôle as married men is invalidated. Part of the laughter is directed at the fact that this world of men with their institutionalised hierarchy of rôles is, in essence, an unreal world, where there is precious little room for the fulfilment of genuine human needs, and especially for the expression of sexuality.

None the less, the humanity of individual figures can be seen lurking behind the restrictions imposed upon them by the rôles they play. In *Lysistrata and NATO* as elsewhere, they are more than mere 'transfer pictures' and anything but drawn in black and white. Just as the weaknesses of the women are often allowed to appear on the surface—they are at times motivated by bitterness, if not plain hatred—so even the 'baddies' among the men are not drawn in a totally negative fashion. The corrupt minister, who begins with threats of murder, falls in love with Lysistrata and by the end of the play is acting in an unmistakeably sympathetic manner towards the women. The same holds true for the Athenians, with the significant exception of Captain Polizoides, who is a supporter of the colonels' junta and the political views it represents. And even the local priest is at times drawn as a sympathetic figure, as when, for example, he allows himself to be persuaded much against his will to support the women in a falsehood, through which he helps to prevent the unfaithfulness of one of their number from being revealed to her husband. (IV,155ff)

Hochhuth's latest play to date follows on naturally from its precedessors. Once more, a privileged individual is driven by his position in society and the possibilities it offers to take action in a moral cause to the benefit of the underprivileged. But it is made clear from the outset that any such action follows its own laws, the laws of pure humanity, as it were, and is therefore in principle not dependent on any man-made laws and, if the circumstances are right, could lead to violation of such laws. The protagonists of Hochhuth's last three plays are all fully conscious of this fact; but even in *Soldiers* Churchill is no mere negative figure, a cold-blooded murderer, but is positively depicted as a man whose actions are directed at peace. His mistake is that, being a man, he finds it impossible to shake off the mode of thinking which the inhuman estranged world of men has imposed upon him when he comes to choose the means to his end. Still, it is hardly easy for him to do other, since he is fighting against the worst that humanity is capable of producing, in the person of Hitler, and so he is convinced that he too is compelled to beat him at his own game, and being the soldier he is, he cannot concieve of any other way of destroying him than by martial means.

Lysistrata and NATO demonstrates an alternative approach, and a real revolution which would put an end to men's wars, and to this end the initiative could only come from women. The central objective of their action is to defeat and root out the worst excesses of the world of men, that artificial, but very powerful hierarchy of rôles, which men hide behind in order to oppress others. Only women are by their very nature still untainted enough to strive towards this objective, and in so doing they employ natural, human 'weapons'. If women were to consider their own strengths and stop subjecting themselves to the laws of men, they might well bring about a fundamental change in society.

Time and again in his plays, Hochhuth causes the spectator to consider a possibility of this kind. With the exception of Peter Weiss, he is the only contemporary German dramatist who has even begun to do anything of the kind in the theatre with any sense of commitment and real determination. If the theatre in West Germany had been more determined and open to experiment it might well have fostered a whole generation of political dramatists against whose works it would be possible for us to make a more objective assessment of Hochhuth's achievement, especially since most of his plays are divided against themselves as we have demonstrated earlier. As long as there is nothing to prove the opposite, it seems probable that the structural imbalances in the plays reflect the essential nature of the kind of problems with which Hochhuth is wrestling. Maybe it is more than the theatre as we know it is capable of, to peep behind the façade of life as it is today, to seek to break down the principal taboos of society, and at the same time to stimulate the spectator to identify himself emotionally with the characters on stage. Even the great Brecht has manifestly failed as a contemporary political writer. And his most significant successors, Frisch and Dürrenmatt, have never really managed to advance further than the somewhat negative position of stating the political realities as they exist here and now. On the other hand, Hochhuth does succeed time and again in shaking himself free of this uncommitted negativity : he makes the spectator become emotionally involved with possible changes in society as portrayed on the stage, which he may find unpleasant, but which at the same time must be thought about. And in this sense at least the theatre is deeply political, for all its manifold weaknesses, and for this reason an essential part of our society.

PART THREE

CONCLUSION

THE IMPACT OF HOCHHUTH

Melchinger wrote these words about the première of Hochhuth's first play on 20 February 1963 :

> The day on which Rolf Hochhuth's play *The Representative* was first performed in the Berlin Volksbühne can be regarded as an historic date. . . . It transported the theatre from a peripheral position into the very heart of contemporary life. . . . The new direction which a large number of dramatists have followed since that 20 February 1963 is a direct result of *The Representative*.[56]

Even Hochhuth's fiercest critics will not deny that Hochhuth made his most forceful impact as a dramatist with his first play. As Melchinger goes on to say, the play showed 'the scriveners of the theatre in no uncertain terms what their fellow men and women wanted to see on the stage', or rather '*how* they wanted to see it.'[57] What *The Representative* did was to bring to the surface a real need on the part of the public which those in charge of the theatre had up until then failed to recognise in the overwhelmingly repressive atmosphere of the years of rebuilding in the early 'sixties and whose presence they would have continued to be in ignorance of, if Piscator had not had the courage to put the play on, and that is the need to be informed more concretely and more comprehensively about the recent past and contemporary events in all their ramifications, and, as a result to be able to consider them in greater depth than was ever possible before.

Hochhuth's play brought out into the open this hunger for the truth at a time when many areas of the truth were, as always tends to happen, made into taboo subjects for a variety of reasons, but also at a time when a new factor had emerged, the mass medium of television which was beginning to bring into people's homes for the very first time an awareness of just how complex and difficult to understand the full truth really is.

At about the same period, it is true, other dramatists had embarked upon a search for the truth about the recent past—for example, Heinar Kipphardt in his war play, *The General's Dog* (1962)—but it was only the sensational success of *The Representative* which demonstrated that the theatre was more than just an important part of the contemporary scene, it could actually influence people. As a result, Kipphardt in his next plays— *In the Matter of J Robert Oppenheimer* and also *Joel Brand*—went completely over to the documentary theatre, and Peter Weiss did not pursue the 'total theatre' of his *Marat/Sade*, first performed in the 1964 season in Berlin, any further, but turned directly to unresolved historical issues (*The Investigation*, *Vietnam Discourse*, and *Trotzky in Exile* (*Trotski im Exil*). Günter Grass followed suit by giving up his flirtation with the Theatre of the Absurd (*The bad Cooks* (*Die bösen Köche*) came out in 1960) and turning in *The Plebeians rehearse the Uprising* (*Die Plebejer proben den Aufstand*) to contemporary issues. And the same is true of Tankred Dorst, who had come into the live theatre via marionettes: after *Poppy* (*Mohn*) in 1963, he produced no more dramatic fantasies, but started working in the same year on *Toller*, his theatrical revue of the Munich soviet republic.

All this, however, does not mean that Hochhuth should be held up as the father of the documentary theatre which came into being after the success of *The Representative*. Werner Mittenzwei writes of Hochhuth's theatre that it

> has nothing—I repeat absolutely nothing—to do with the direction taken by the documentary theatre, least of all was he its founder. . . . In accordance with his conception of the individual, he is mainly concerned to seek out the biographical elements in historical material.[58]

And it is this very tendency which is taken further in many plays by the dramatists we have already quoted, and others—for example, in Weiss's *Trotsky* and *Hölderlin* plays, to some extent in Kipphardt's *Joel Brand*, and unmistakeably in Dorst's *Toller*. Both these factors—the interest in historical material and in the historical individual—are clearly reflections of the selfsame unconditional pursuit of the truth about contemporary historical issues, in which *The Representative* led the way for the theatre in West Germany. In 1963, Karl Jaspers stated of this search that

> everything is hushed up, veiled in secrecy and we cannot see where we are going. Hochhuth demands of us that we should be open, and take the issues seriously, even in the eyes of God.[59]

The scandals which attend so many performances of the play underline the fact that, at his first attempt at being a playwright, Hochhuth touched on an open nerve of the time and seemingly contradicted current attitudes. While people as a whole may hunger after the truth, there are any number of folk who must find it intolerable to search for something which threatens their psychological defence systems. Night after night in Basle the police had to be out in force to protect the audience from the actions of enraged demonstrators. It was the same in Paris; *Der Spiegel* described the events accompanying the presentation of *The Representative* in the *Théâtre de l'Athénée* in these terms :

> The cries of fury ('Outrageous!'; 'Filthy lies!'; 'Dirty swine!') swelled to a climax ... stink-bombs were thrown, tomatoes flew through the air, rotten eggs were smashed, demonstrators were stamping and shouting in the foyer. They were trampling about in the stalls and yelling on the stage, and the poor actor playing the Pope was wasting his breath when he came down to the footlights with a gesture of benediction and exhorted the public thus : 'Please, I beg you, I'm just exercising my craft here!'[60]

In New York supporters of the local Nazi party paraded in SA uniforms in front of the theatre. And *Newsweek* was sufficiently impressed to observe that this writer Hochhuth 'could lay claim ... to the title of the world's most important dramatist'.[61]

The play also exercised the minds of governments :

> The Foreign Office was not just approached directly about the displeasure of the Vatican at the silence of the Federal government over Hochhuth's drama. There were also semi-official expressions of astonishment on the part of the Belgian and Italian governments at the performance of *The Representative* in Germany and the Federal government's failure to make a statement about it.[62]

A motion to this effect was put down by the foreign affairs working party of the CDU/CSU in the Federal parliament and immediately received a reply regretting the situation. In 1963 alone four books came out at the same time containing opinions about the play : reviews, essays, letters, newspaper articles, statements by representatives of the Church. In the following year, a similar book was published in the United States.[63]

This, of course, meant a very pleasant success for Hochhuth himself, in that any theatre in the world would put on anything else he cared to write. The other side of the coin is the fact, which Hochhuth himself has stressed, that his play was not much of a success in Germany itself, since it only received eight productions in the west (in contrast to the east, where it received thirteen). West German television has so far not shown a single play by Hochhuth (although there was a dramatisation of *The Berlin Antigone* done by Leopold Ahlsen), whilst in other countries—in Belgium, Jugoslavia, the GDR, and in English-speaking countries—there have been many television productions of his plays.

Particularly when he challenges taboos, Hochhuth's uncompromising search for the truth tends to arouse extreme reactions; great enthusiasm on the one hand, but great fears on the other. And these fears give rise to the violent aggression characteristic of the furore surrounding the productions of his work such as we have already described. By and large, it took the critics longer than anyone else to achieve that level of unrestrained aggression. None the less, Hochhuth's later plays continued to pursue his unorthodox search for the truth and for the proper path to be taken in order to bring about change in society, and also his unmasking of ossified modes of conduct and social rôles. This fact probably explains the tidal wave of opprobrium which rose with increasing fury from the columns of the weekend supplements. Ludwig Marcuse, 'shocked at the hatred' which he saw in the press conference and reviews which attended the première of *Soldiers*, asked if they were 'whipping up a witch-hunt of some kind'.[64] A further reflection of the venom generated by this play is the fact that the British censor banned it, shortly before his office was done away with, and that Hochhuth himself had to pay heavy damages as a result of assertions made in the text.[65]

But things went further than that: *Guerillas* also sparked off critical onslaughts which were as vicious as they were unsubstantiated, and not just in the United States itself. *The Midwife* led, among other things, to charges being laid against Hochhuth on grounds of stirring up national hatred. Werner Mittenzwei, writing for the GDR public, explains to them what is a matter of general knowledge to everyone in the west: 'The attitude of critics in the press towards Hochhuth's plays has become increasingly harsh and negative in recent years.'[66] Mittenzwei goes on to describe how the press avoided trying to challenge this well-informed and widely read dramatist; instead,

> they sought to destroy him on aesthetic grounds. There was no lack of articles trying to demonstrate that Hochhuth's conception of drama was hopelessly out-moded, that his manner of presentation often bordered on the banal, that he was describing the international political arena with childish naïveté, and so forth.[67]

What all these attacks on Hochhuth have in common is the fact that they fail to do any justice to the essential qualities of his plays, and the reason for this is that, for the most part, they are not concerned with the plays at all, but clearly simply with cutting down to size a man whom they evidently regard in some indefinable manner as posing a threat of some kind to them.

From his own experience, Hochhuth has good grounds

for complaining that 'it doesn't exactly make one happy to be alive if one is born to be a writer in a German-speaking country'. (III,472) He is referring here to the prevalent official attitude towards writers in the Federal Republic, which he pillories in an open letter on this subject called 'Our "written-off" writers in the Federal Republic'. (III,335–46) And, indeed, it has scarcely been possible for the authorities to ignore him, as the reaction of Chancellor Ludwig Erhard to his 1965 'Class War' essay amply demonstrates. The continuing impact of Hochhuth's plays and essays, then, operates on two levels and in two conflicting directions. On the one hand, his success has from the very outset led the German political theatre into new directions, but on the other this very success has caused him to be regarded very much as a dubious character. He continues to be held up to ridicule for polemicising without getting his facts right, for an 'excess of zeal', or for artistic or dramatical incompetence.

For all that, critics who are not totally blinded by their prejudices are obliged to admit time and again, like Ulrich Schreiber in his not over friendly discussion of *Lysistrata*, that 'Hochhuth is the internationally most successful dramatist in the Federal Republic, who is second only to Brecht in raising the German theatre to a position of world importance.'[68] Schreiber states that Hochhuth's *The Representative* had a more general impact than a single drama normally has : 'Like Peter Weiss, Hochhuth was also the leader of a new movement which, in the train of the 1968 May troubles in Paris, brought into being the nostalgia wave.'[69] It is true that *Guerillas*, like Weiss's *Hölderlin*, showed the way to plays like Gaston Salvatore's *Büchner's Death* (*Büchners Tod*), but it is open to question whether this movement really can be attributed to one individual dramatist. It is more probably a result of the disillusionment that set in after 1968–1969, which itself has now been reflected in the theatre. But what distinguishes Hochhuth especially is the fact that, unlike Salvatore, for example, he does not end with resignation, but carries on the fight for a more just society and, as the comedies demonstrate, he keeps on working out new ways of continuing that fight.

Only the future can show whether others will follow on in his footsteps. At the present time, in the middle of the 'seventies, the German theatre is more or less stagnant, as it has long been, and hostile to any kind of innovation or experimentation. *The Representative* has continued to exercise an influence on the political theatre for a decade after its first appearance; but the importance of Hochhuth's work extends beyond both his first play and beyond his plays as drama. The achievement of a writer is not invariably restricted to what we are pleased to call 'literature'. Hochhuth is well aware of this fact: in his 1975 Thomas Mann essay, he asks if a speech is not also a 'work', if it is 'less enduring than a short story, or a ballad'.[70]

It would be a good thing for the Germans if Hochhuth created a great following with the ideas which his work, and in particular his essays and letters, contain—his positive relationship towards history, his demand for individual responsibility, and his lack of concern for the prevalent trends and opinions. But, for all its desirability, it is not particularly likely in a country and at a time when the only way for an aspiring young man to get on in his job is to conform with the conventions and act the willing subordinate.

What sets Hochhuth apart is this courage to challenge the authorities that mould public opinion, whenever he feels it necessary to do so; and it is this which has caused him to be on the receiving end of more fame and obloquy than nearly anyone else of his time, and will continue to do so in the thinking of all those who come into contact with him, whether they are aware of it or not. In the short term, there may well be no successor to Hochhuth's uncompromising and unrelenting pursuit of his objectives. But, in future generations, whenever a subject is raised which might cause a scandal or touch on a taboo subject, people might still say that there is material for a Hochhuth play. And such plays as Hochhuth himself may write in the future are assured of an attentive audience.

NOTES

1 'Mein Lieber. Ein Brief von Dieter Vollbrecht', in: 'Der Streit um Hochhuths *Stellvertreter*', *Theater unserer Zeit.* (V,15)

2 'Thomas Mann oder der Undank vom Urenkel', *Der Spiegel*, no. 24 (1975), pp. 130–1.

3 'Der Streit um Hochhuths *Stellvertreter*', p. 17.

4 P. Wolff-Windegg, '*Der Stellvertreter* im Basler Stadttheater', *Basler Nachrichten*, 25.9.63.

5 *Die Berliner Antigone. Prosa und Verse*, Reinbeck bei Hamburg, 1975, pp. 100–2.

6 G. Rühle, 'Aufwind für das Drama', *Frankfurter Allgemeine Zeitung*, 5.9.1962.

7 'Zu *Soldaten*: Gegen die *Neue Züricher Zeitung*'. (I,194–5)

8 *ibid.*, p. 194.

9 See also S. Melchinger, *Hochhuth*, Hannover, 1967, p. 26.

10 Interview with Hochhuth, 12.1.1971.

11 *ibid.*

12 J. Kaiser, 'Drei Schwierigkeiten beim Schreiben des Dramas', in: J. Schondorff (ed.), *Junges Deutsches Theater von heute,* Munich, 1961, p. 13.

13 'Zu *Soldaten*'. (I,193)

14 'Der alte Mythos vom "neuen Menschen".' (III,352–425)

15 Interview with Hochhuth, 12.1.1971.

16 Interview with Ludwig Erhard on the occasion of his seventy-fifth birthday (6.2.1972), North German Television. The interview makes it clear that Erhard

was specifically referring to Hochhuth and no one else in this context.

17 'Die Diskussion des Aufrufs zum Klassenkampf'. (I,73)

18 The essay 'Der alte Mythos vom "neuen Menschen" ,' published in Volume III of the Rowohlt edition, contains both the original 1969 version (originally in *Konkret*, 18.9.1969, under the title 'Hört nicht auf Marcuse') and the expanded version written in 1971.

19 Interview with Hochhuth, 12.1.1971.

20 It is interesting to record that Hermann H. Kamps, in his speech during the prize-giving ceremony, felt it necessary to excuse himself : 'Even those who see many things quite differently from this writer and would express them in a different way are bound to admit that here there is a man at work who is striving to take a passionate hold of the raw material of history, to concentrate it and translate it into tangible dramatic terms.' *Der Stellvertreter*, Reinbeck bei Hamburg, 1963, p. 274.

21 Golo Mann, 'Die eigentliche Leistung', *Basler Nachrichten*, 17.9.63. (quoted from II,248)

22 H. E. Holthusen, for example : 'The subject cannot truly be mastered, neither artistically, nor in human terms, neither emotionally nor intellectually.' Letter to Hochhuth, 19.2.1963, in : F. J. Raddatz (ed.), *Summa iniuria oder Durfte der Papst schweigen? Hochhuths 'Stellvertreter' in der öffentlichen Kritik*, Reinbeck bei Hamburg, 1963, p. 22.

23 Walter Muschg, 'Hochhuth und Lessing'. (II,286)

24 B. Brecht, 'Das epische Theater', in : *Schriften zum Theater*, III, Frankfurt, 1963, p. 55.

25 P. Szondi, *Theorie des modernen Dramas*, Frankfurt, 1963, pp. 14ff.

26 *ibid.*, p. 55.

27 Differences in the list of dramatis personae between the collected works and the separately published play are attributable to typographical errors.

28 See Melchinger, p. 25.

29 In a letter to Hochhuth, 9.4.1963, in: 'Der Streit um Hochhuths *Stellvertreter*', p. 21.

30 In a letter to Hochhuth, 19.2.1963, in: *Summa iniuria* . . ., p. 23.

31 R. C. Zimmermann, 'Hochhuths *Stellvertreter* und die Tradition der pamphletischen Literatur', in: 'Der Streit um Hochhuths *Stellvertreter*, pp. 164ff.

32 'Pius XII und die Pforten der Hölle. Joachim Kaiser über die Diskussion der Katholischen Akademie in München', in: 'Der Streit um Hochhuths *Stellvertreter*', p. 122.

33 D. Irving, *Moskaus Staatsräson? Sikorski und Churchill—eine tragische Allianz*, Munich, 1969. (An expanded version of the original English edition, *Accident. The Death of General Sikorsky*, London, 1967.)

34 'Hochhuths neue Provokation: Luftkrieg ist Verbrechen', *Theater heute*, no. 2 (1967), p. 8.

35 For example, Karl-Heinz Janssen, 'Hochhuth als Historiker', *Die Zeit*, 20.10.1967.

36 First published in extract form in *Theater heute*, no. 2 (1967). (Complete text in I,106–29 under the title 'Vom Soldaten zum Berufsverbrecher'.)

37 See Melchinger, 'Hochhuths neue Provokation', p. 6.

38 *Die Zeit*, 24.5.1968.

39 See the report 'Der Pessimist im Dorfkrug', *Die Zeit*, 22.12.1967, and the letter from Wolf-Heinrich Schmidt ('Wie politisches Theater nicht sein darf') which appeared in a subsequent issue.

40 Interview with Hochhuth, 12.1.1971.

41 '*Guerillas* gesehen von Peter Hensel', in: 'Schiller,

Hochhuth und die Polit-Burleske', *Die Weltwoche*, 22.5.1970.

42 Interview with Hochhuth, 12.1.1971.

43 H. Karasek, 'In der Dramaturgie ein Klassizist', *Die Zeit*, 22.5.1970.

44 V. Marchetti and J. D. Marks, *The CIA and the Cult of Intelligence*, New York, 1974.

45 *ibid.*, p. 244.

46 G. Hensel, *Die Weltwoche*, 22.5.1970.

47 G. G. Eckstein, 'Zu Hochhuths *Guerillas*: eine amerikanische Stimme', *Merkur*, vol. 24. no. 10 (1970), p. 996.

48 K. Tynan, 'Sabotage in hohen Sphären' (account of the prevention of the production of *Soldiers* by the censor in 1967), *Soldaten*, Reinbeck bei Hamburg, 1970, p. 190.

49 H. Karasek, 'In Hochhuths Kreißsaal', *Die Zeit*, 12.5.1972.

50 *ibid.*

51 By this, Hochhuth seeks to underline the fact that the SPD has no monopoly of social reforms, as he says in the play: 'For all that the CDU has / a left wing—the SPD only a / left past'. (III,179)

52 *Die Zeit*, 12.5.1972.

53 R. Voss, 'Wieso schreibt Hochhuth aus provinzieller Rechthaberei', letter to the editor in *Die Zeit*, 26.5.1972.

54 This study is based on the original version which appeared in 1973. The more recent version has been considerably shortened, because the cast list was too long in the original.

55 The source is the German version, published as *Der weibliche Eunuch. Aufruf zur Befreiung der Frau*, Frankfurt, 1971.

56 Melchinger, 'Hochhuths neue Provokation', p. 8.

57 *ibid.*, p. 17.
58 W. Mittenzwei, 'Die vereinsamte Position eines Erfolgreichen. Der Weg des Dramatikers Rolf Hochhuth', *Sinn und Form* XXVI (1974), p. 1265.
59 Radio Basle, 10.11.1963. Quoted from *Programmheft Stellvertreter 1972*.
60 *Der Spiegel*, no. 52 (1963).
61 Quoted from the cover of Volume II.
62 *Der Spiegel*, no. 20 (1963).
63 In addition to those cited in the bibliography : H. R. Tschopp-Brunner, 'Hochhuth und kein Ende', privately printed, Basle, 1963.
64 L. Marcuse, 'Hochhuth und seine Verächter', II, p. 476.
65 'In England, Hochhuth did not get away with his picture of Churchill—it was branded as libellous. . . . The Czech pilot of the plane, in which Sikorsky crashed, Edvard Prchal, sued him and Hochhuth was ordered to pay £50,000 damages'. *Die Zeit*, 12.5.1972.
66 Mittenzwei, p. 1268.
67 *ibid.*
68 U. Schrieber, 'Die neue Lysistrate. Hochhuth und das politische Theater', *Merkur*, vol. 30. no. 5 (1974), pp. 488ff.
69 *ibid.*, p. 489.
70 'Thomas Mann oder der Undank vom Urenkel', *Der Spiegel*, no. 24 (1975), p. 131.

BIBLIOGRAPHY

I WORKS BY HOCHHUTH

The principal edition consulted, published by Rowohlt, Reinbeck bei Hamburg, is as follows:

I = *Krieg und Klassenkrieg. Studien.* Foreword by F. J. Raddatz. 1971.

II = *Dramen (Der Stellvertreter, Soldaten, Guerillas).* (With essays by Clive Barnes, Jack Kroll, Golo Mann, Ludwig Marcuse, Walter Muschg, Erwin Piscator, H. C. N. Williams.) 1972.

III = *Die Hebamme, Komödie. Erzählungen, Gedichte, Essays.* 1971.

IV = *Lysistrate und die NATO, Komödie. Mit einer Studie: Frauen und Mütter, Bachofen und Germaine Greer.* 1973.

Other editions of Hochhuth's works (all published by Rowohlt):

Der Stellvertreter, Schauspiel. Mit einem Vorwort von Erwin Piscator, 1963.

Der Stellvertreter, Ein christliches Trauerspiel. Mit einem Vorwort von Erwin Piscator und einem Essay von Walter Muschg, 1967.

Die Berliner Antigone, Novelle, 1965. (First published in *Frankfurter Allgemeine Zeitung,* 20.4.1963.)

Soldaten, Nekrolog auf Genf, Tragödie, 1967. (Paperback edition 1970.)

Guerillas, Tragödie, 1970. (Paperback edition 1972.)

Die Hebamme, Komödie, 1973. (Revised version.)

Zwischenspiel in Baden-Baden, 1974. (Extended version of *Resignation oder die Geschichte einer Ehe*, 1959.)

Lysistrate und die NATO, Komödie, 1976. (Revised version.)

Die Berliner Antigone, Prosa und Verse, 1976. (Includes four poems published for the first time.)

Also quoted:

R. Taëni, interview with Rolf Hochhuth, 12.1.1971. Published in English in a shortened form under the title 'Revolution by Infiltration', *Meanjin Quarterly*, XXX, no. 1 (1971).

'Thomas Mann oder der Undank vom Urenkel. Rolf Hochhuth zu Hanjo Kestings zehn polemischen Thesen', *Der Spiegel*, no. 24 (1975).

II PRINCIPAL WORKS ON HOCHHUTH

F. J. Raddatz (ed.), *Summa iniuria oder Durfte der Papst schweigen? Hochhuths 'Stellvertreter' in der öffentlichen Kritik*, Reinbeck bei Hamburg, 1963.

Der Streit um Hochhuths 'Stellvertreter', Theater unserer Zeit, vol 5, Basle, 1963.

W. Adolph, *Verfälschte Geschichte. Antwort an Rolf Hochhuth*, Berlin, 1963.

E. Bentley (ed.), *The Storm over the Deputy. Essays and Articles about Hochhuth's explosive Drama*, New York, 1964.

S. Melchinger, *Hochhuth*, Dramatiker des Welttheaters, vol 4, Hannover, 1967.

'Eine Dokumentation zum *Stellvertreter*', *Programmheft 'Stellvertreter'*, Swiss Touring Theatre, 1972. (Produced by R. D. Macdonald and Rolf Hochhuth.)